YOUTH
PROTECTION

How to Protect Your Children From Child Abuse:
A Parent's Guide

BOY SCOUTS OF AMERICA

DEAR PARENT

The Boy Scouts of America is pleased to provide this booklet—it might be the most important information you, your child, and your family will ever read. Understanding these pages could prevent your child or another child from being abused or may empower you to stop abuse as soon as possible and seek the necessary help.

Child abuse is something we would rather not talk about, or even think about, but we must. Every offender benefits from our ignorance. If we fail to do everything we can to keep our children safe, the consequences can be devastating, even deadly.

This booklet cannot address all threats to personal safety your child may experience in and out of Scouting, but it will teach you how to identify and prevent numerous forms of abuse. It contains exercises, based on a set of personal safety rules, that will empower your child to better recognize, respond to, and report abuse. Go through the exercises together. **Your child is that important**. In fact, all children are that important. **Youth Protection Begins With YOU**.

Using This Booklet

This booklet is divided into two sections. The first section contains information for parents about child abuse and some tips for talking with your child about child abuse. The second section contains exercises for you to share with your child. Research shows that children whose parents talk to them about preventing abuse are better able to protect themselves and are more likely to tell if they are abused.

As your child grows, look for opportunities to continue a dialogue about personal safety awareness. Open communication gives children the reassurance that no matter how frightening something may be, their parents are there to help.

WHAT EVERY PARENT SHOULD KNOW

Children can experience abuse in many ways: neglect, physical abuse, sexual abuse, or emotional abuse. Often a child who is abused in one way is abused in multiple ways. When we protect a child from one form of abuse, such as physical abuse, we are often protecting the child from additional forms of abuse.

Neglect

Neglect often involves depriving a child of food, clothing, shelter, medical care, or other necessities of life. Neglect can also involve exposing a child to harmful substances or materials, such as drugs, alcohol, or pornography, or to harmful practices such as violent behavior.

Parents who cannot provide for children as a result of poverty are not committing neglect. Neglect is a deliberate act or inaction that has a physical and emotional impact on a child and, in some instances, can cost a child his or her life.

A number of clues suggest that a child might be neglected. The child who frequently comes to meetings with body odor, the child who is frequently unkempt, the child who is living in a dangerous environment, and the child with an obvious medical need that goes unattended all are exhibiting signs of potential neglect. So is the child who is always hungry or who hoards or steals food, the child who is seldom dressed appropriately for the weather, and the child who regularly talks of seeing a parent drunk or bruised from being hit.

Any time a child exhibits a need or condition that a reasonable parent would attend to—especially when the failure to provide the need impairs the child's physical or emotional well-being—the child is likely being neglected.

Physical Abuse

Physical abuse is the deliberate injury of a child by a person responsible for the child's care.

Physical abuse injuries can include bruises, broken bones, burns, and abrasions. Children experience minor injuries as a normal part of childhood, usually in places such as the shins, knees, and elbows. When injuries are found in the soft-tissue areas on the abdomen or back, or when they do not seem to be typical childhood injuries, it is possible that the child has been abused.

Blows to the stomach may result in abdominal bruises, even if there is not a visible mark. When a child complains of pain or indicates having been punched in the stomach, such a complaint should be taken seriously, given the possibility of internal injury.

The following signs are commonly associated with abuse but are not absolutes.

- Injuries the child or parent cannot adequately explain
- Injuries on a child who has been absent
- Complaints of soreness when moving
- Fear of going home with or to parents

Talking to Youth About Suspicious Injuries

It is appropriate to ask a child about suspicious injuries. If the child tells of abuse or gives an answer that does not make sense given the location or extent of injuries, you should document this statement and immediately contact the local law enforcement agency or state department of children and family services.

For more information about reporting requirements, call 911 or see the Child Welfare Information Gateway website at www.childwelfare.gov for your state hotline number.

Sexual Abuse

When an adult or older youth uses his or her authority to involve a child in sexual activity, it is child sexual abuse. Sexual abuse includes any activity performed for the sexual satisfaction of the offender. Children can be at risk of sexual abuse anywhere access and opportunity present such as: at home; at a neighbor's house; at school, field trips, and public events; and in Scouting.

A common misconception about sexual abuse is that children are most likely to be abused by strangers. In fact, a sex offender is usually someone the child knows and trusts. Sex offenders are most often male, but females also can be offenders.

Sexual Abuse by Adults

Adults who abuse children may manipulate, bribe, coerce, threaten, or force a child into feeling like a partner in the sexual activity. They most often use a multistep "grooming" process that focuses on the child's needs and possibly on the child's parents as well. The sex offender might offer the parents free babysitting services, for example, or make friends with them to gain enough trust to be alone with the child.

Once the sex offender has identified the target child, characteristically, the grooming process moves to seemingly harmless touching, such as hugging, massages, and exposure, and seeking opportunities to be alone with the child. The sex offender usually seeks a child who craves affection or attention and makes that child feel special by spending a lot of time with him or her and giving gifts and money. All children are vulnerable to sexual abuse because of their innocence, naivete, and total trust in and dependence upon adults.

A red flag might be a person who violates the BSA's Youth Protection policy of no one-on-one contact and seeks one-on-one contact with youth in or out of Scouting.

When the sex offender senses that the child has been sufficiently conditioned to physical contact and has an emotional bond, the physical contact becomes more intrusive. The offender may prey on the child's emerging curiosity about sexuality and may carry on under the guise of sex education or playing inappropriate games. It may involve violating rules, drinking alcohol, smoking cigarettes— all to create a "special relationship."

Most children do not know they are being groomed into inappropriate behavior until it is too late.

Many offenders are clever enough to manipulate the child into believing that he or she is equally to blame or will not be believed if they tell. Many children feel trapped and are afraid to tell.

Sexual Abuse by Other Youth

It is also possible for a child of the same age to abuse another through force or manipulation. About a third of sexual abuse occurs at the hands of other children, including older youth and youth in positions to manipulate through bullying behavior using their size or knowledge difference. Any peer activity, such as a club initiation, in which sexual activity is included is a form of sexual abuse. Overnight activities pose a greater risk of abuse. Personal safety awareness rules should be reviewed before these activities. Adults who learn or discover that youth-on-youth abuse has occurred must take immediate steps to stop it.

Emotional Abuse

A child suffers from emotional abuse when continually ridiculed, blamed, humiliated, or compared unfavorably with others. Emotional abuse damages the child's self-esteem. Studies find that emotional abuse is just as harmful as, if not more harmful than, other forms of maltreatment. It can lead to developmental problems, speech delays, depression, anxiety, and conditions such as low empathy and difficulty with peers.

Emotional abuse can occur when a parent completely ignores or rejects or regularly threatens to beat a child or when a child struggles to meet a parent's unreasonable expectations in academics, athletics, or other areas. Emotional abuse can also result if an adult or older youth provides a child with alcohol, drugs, pornography, or other harmful substances or materials.

Spiritual Abuse

An often-overlooked form of child maltreatment is spiritual abuse—the incorporation of religion into the abuse of a child. Some studies suggest that sex offenders are particularly attracted to faith communities because they find clergy and other faith leaders to be overly trusting. If your child is active in a faith community, make sure it has rigorous child protection policies in place.

Bullying

Bullying is an intentional, aggressive behavior, often involving an imbalance of power or strength, that usually is repeated over a period of time. Bullying can take many forms, including hitting or punching, teasing or name calling, intimidating use of gestures or social exclusion, or sending insulting messages by phone or computer (cyberbullying). Victims of bullying behavior are more likely to be depressed, have low self-esteem, be absent from school or other activities, feel sick, or think about suicide.

Any information indicating a youth has mentioned or talked about suicide must be taken seriously and reported to a responsible leader, law enforcement, or suicide hotline (National Suicide Prevention Lifeline, www.suicidepreventionlifeline.org, 800-273-8255). If your child is being targeted, do not blame your child or tell him or her to ignore the behavior or engage in physical retaliation. Instead, listen carefully and report the bullying behavior to the people responsible for the program where bullying is occurring. For more information, please see the BSA's Bullying Awareness webpage at www.scouting.org/Training/YouthProtection/bullying.aspx.

Internet/Social Media Safety

Parents play a critical role in keeping children safe from those who use the internet and social media to access and harm children. Parents can limit the danger by setting basic guidelines such as when children go online, what sites they can visit, and regular check-ins to see and discuss the choices that are being made with technology. Today's youth are spending more time than ever using digital media for education, research, socializing, and fun. To help families and volunteers keep youth safe while online, the BSA introduced the Cyber Chip. In developing this tool, the BSA teamed up with content expert NetSmartz®, part of the National Center for Missing and Exploited Children® and training expert for many law enforcement agencies. Earning the Cyber Chip is a requirement for all Cub Scout ranks except Bobcat. For more information, please see the BSA's Cyber Chip webpage at www.scouting.org/Training/YouthProtection/CyberChip.aspx and NCMEC's Netsmartz website at www.netsmartz.org.

Youth With Developmental Disabilities

Children with disabilities or behavioral problems are at greater risk of abuse than other children simply because offenders often target children they believe will be least likely to report abuse. Accordingly, while it is important to teach all children to recognize would-be abusers and to tell a trusted adult about abuse, this message is particularly important for children with disabilities.

Signs Your Child Might Have Been Abused

The best indicator of abuse is a disclosure by your child that someone hurt or scared him or her, or made him or her feel uncomfortable. Unfortunately, many children never speak of abuse, so it is important for you to have ongoing conversations with your child about personal safety and to give repeated reminders that he or she can tell you anything.

If your child is abused by a parent, relative, sibling, or someone else close to you, it may be particularly difficult for him or her to disclose abuse to you and also difficult for you to accept. Studies show that children rarely lie about sexual abuse or other maltreatment. Accordingly, if your child discloses abuse or even expresses discomfort with a particular person or situation, always take that as your cue to act. Children communicate with us through their language, their behaviors, and their emotions. Communication about abuse is often subtle and indirect. A child may offer a disguised disclosure, saying something like, "I have a friend who ...," in an attempt to gauge how an adult will react. The child who receives a helpful or sympathetic response is more likely to disclose any abuse experiences.

Each child's response to abuse is unique. Signs of stress frequently accompany maltreatment, but stress can have many causes. Other possible indicators of abuse include

- Sudden withdrawal from activities the child previously enjoyed
- Reluctance to be around a particular individual, especially in the absence of others
- Changes in behavior or in school performance, including lower grades
- Inability to focus or learning problems with no known cause
- Hypervigilance (excessive watchfulness as if anticipating something bad happening)
- Overly compliant behavior or an excessive desire to please

In addition, a child being sexually victimized may

- Have difficulty sitting or walking
- Complain of pain or itching in the genital or anal areas
- Use sexually explicit language or act out sexual behavior inappropriate for his or her age

---

Speaking With a Child Who Discloses or Indicates Abuse

When speaking with a child who discloses or indicates abuse, your role is to become the trusted adult. A good approach includes the following:

- Be an upstander; get involved.
- If you see something, stop it.
- If you know or suspect something, report it.
- If you are not sure, seek advice from an expert.

If a child does disclose abuse, it is important that adults respond calmly and in a supportive manner. Avoid statements that might indicate shame, blame, disbelief, disgust, or fear. If the abuse started or occurred much earlier, avoid asking a child why he or she did not tell anyone sooner. Tell the child it wasn't his or her fault, and express belief in the child's disclosure by simply stating, "I believe you." This will further support and validate the child's statement. Avoid asking children for detailed information. Ask basic, open-ended questions to discern the following information:

- Name and address of the alleged victim, if known
- Name and address of the alleged offender, if known
- Location of the alleged abuse
- Nature (e.g., sexual, physical, emotional) and extent of the alleged abuse
- Approximate date of the last incident (if an older child)

Adults should recognize that talking with children about maltreatment, especially sexual abuse, is not natural or comfortable for anyone; however, a child's first disclosure—and your response—may have lasting effects. If the child senses you do not want to hear about his or her experiences or senses that he or she is saying something wrong, the child might shut down. Simply let the child know that you believe him or her, you care, it wasn't his or her fault, and you want to help.

The BSA's Barriers to Abuse

You should expect your child's Cub Scout pack to follow the Youth Protection policies put in place by the BSA to provide additional safety for your child and all who are involved in Scouting. These policies also protect adult leaders from the rare possibility of a false report. Scout leaders who are in positions of youth leadership and supervision outside of the Scouting program should follow these practices in those roles as well. You should discuss these policies with your child, so that you, your child, and leaders have a shared understanding of what is expected in Scouting.

Two-deep leadership on all trips and outings is required.
At minimum, two registered adult leaders, or one registered
leader and a participating Scout's parent or another adult, are
required for all trips and outings. One of these adults must be
21 years of age or older. All youth need to know that adults
are there if needed. When the program has all female youth, at
least one adult female, 18 years of age or older, who is Youth
Protection–trained must be present.

**One-on-one contact between adults and youth members is
prohibited.** In situations requiring a personal conference, the
meeting is to be conducted with the knowledge and in view of
other adults and/or youth.

**Two-deep leadership and no one-on-one contact between adults
and youth members includes digital communication.** Leaders
may not have one-on-one private online communications or
engage one-on-one in other digital activities (games, social media,
etc.) with youth members. Leaders should copy a parent and
another leader in digital and online communication, ensuring no
one-on-one contact exists in text, social media, or other forms of
online or digital communication.

**Age-appropriate and separate accommodations for adults and
Scouts are required.** *Tenting.* When camping, no one is permitted
to sleep in the tent of a person of the opposite sex or an adult other
than his or her own spouse, parent, or guardian. Assigning youth
members more than two years apart in age to sleep in the same
tent should be avoided unless the youth are relatives. ***Shower
Facilities.*** Whenever possible, separate shower and latrine facilities
should be provided for male/female adults and male/female youth.
If separate facilities are not available, separate shower times should
be scheduled and posted.

The buddy system should be used at all times. The buddy system
is a safety measure for all Scouting activities. Buddies should
know and be comfortable with each other. Self-selection with
no more than two years difference in age and the same level
of maturity should be strongly encouraged. When necessary,
a buddy team may consist of three Scouts. No youth should
ever be forced into or made to feel uncomfortable by a
buddy assignment.

Privacy of youth is respected. Adult leaders and youth must respect each other's privacy, especially in situations such as changing clothes and taking showers at camp. Adults may enter youth changing or showering areas only to the extent that health and safety requires. Adults must protect their own privacy in similar situations.

Inappropriate use of smartphones, cameras, or imaging or digital devices is prohibited. Although most Scouts and leaders use cameras and other imaging devices responsibly, it is easy to unintentionally or inadvertently invade the privacy of other individuals. The use of any device capable of recording or transmitting visual images in or near shower houses, restrooms, or other areas where privacy is expected is inappropriate.

No secret organizations. The BSA does not recognize any secret organization as part of its program. All aspects of the Scouting program are open to observation by parents and leaders.

Youth leadership is monitored by adult leaders. Adult leaders must monitor and guide the leadership techniques used by youth leaders and ensure that BSA policies are followed.

Discipline must be constructive. Discipline used in Scouting must be constructive and reflect Scouting's values. Corporal punishment is never permitted. Disciplinary activities involving isolation, humiliation, or ridicule are prohibited. Examples of positive discipline include verbal praise and high fives.

Appropriate attire is required for all activities. Proper clothing for activities is required.

No hazing. Physical hazing and initiations are prohibited and may not be included as part of any Scouting activity.

No bullying. Verbal, physical, and cyberbullying are prohibited in Scouting.

All adult leaders and youth members have responsibility. Everyone is responsible for acting in accordance with the Scout Oath and Scout Law. Physical violence, sexual activity, emotional abuse, spiritual abuse, unauthorized weapons, hazing, discrimination, harassment, initiation rites, bullying, cyberbullying, theft, verbal insults, drugs, alcohol, or pornography have no place in the Scouting program and may result in revocation of membership. For more information, please see the BSA's *Guide to Safe Scouting* and other Youth Protection resources.

Reporting Child Abuse and Violations of Policies

All persons involved in Scouting are required to report Youth Protection–related incidents.

Mandatory Report of Child Abuse. All persons involved in Scouting shall report to local law enforcement any good-faith suspicion or belief that any child is or has been physically or sexually abused, physically or emotionally neglected, exposed to any form of violence or threat, or exposed to any form of sexual exploitation, including the possession, manufacture, or distribution of child pornography, online solicitation, enticement, or showing of obscene material. No person may abdicate this reporting responsibility to any other person. For more information, please see your state's reporting statutes on the Child Welfare Information Gateway website at www.childwelfare.gov/systemwide/laws_policies/state/.

Parents Reporting Violations of BSA Youth Protection Policies. If you have reason to believe any of the BSA's Youth Protection policies have been violated, including mandatory reporting of abuse of a child, contact the Scouts First Helpline at 844-726-8871 or scouts1st@scouting.org to report the violation.

If an adult leader or someone else in Scouting is trying to convince your child that his or her advancements or awards are solely dependent on that person's approval, or if that person is asking your child to do anything that seems inappropriate, please immediately contact your Scout executive.

Scouts First Helpline. The BSA has established a 24/7 helpline to receive reports of suspected abuse or behavior that might put a youth at risk, including violations of Youth Protection policies. If you are in doubt as to what action you should take or who you should contact to make a report, please contact the Scouts First Helpline at 844-726-8871 or scouts1st@scouting.org so appropriate action may be taken for the safety of Scouts.

Scouting-Required Steps to Reporting Child Abuse*

1. Ensure the child is in a safe environment.
2. In cases of child abuse or medical emergencies, call 911 immediately. In addition, if the suspected abuse is in the Scout's home or family, you are required to contact the local child protective services office.
3. Notify the Scout executive or the executive's designee during his or her absence. (Contact names and telephone numbers can be found using the BSA local council locator at www.scouting.org/LocalCouncilLocator.aspx)

*State laws may vary.

EXERCISES ON PERSONAL SAFETY AWARENESS

Now that you understand the scope of the problem and how the BSA is working to keep children safe, let us focus on helping you empower your child. Concerned and connected caregivers are a strong component of all child abuse prevention strategies. You have an important role to play in prevention!

Many parents find it difficult to talk with their child about abuse. However, it is important to provide a foundation for a child to understand body ownership and encouragement to come to you with questions and concerns. The personal safety exercises in this section, to be used in conversations with your child, will help you with this process.

Five Topics to Cover With Children

NOTE: Completing the exercises described within these pages fulfills the requirements for your Cub Scout to earn his or her badge or rank and must be completed for each rank earned.

Network of Trusted Adults

Young people should have at least five adults you have identified to whom they can talk freely about their feelings and problems and who provide healthy attention and affection. A child who has such a network of trusted adults will be more difficult for a sex offender to groom. The list of five adults might change depending on the child's circumstances. Prior to Scouting or other activities, parents should discuss with their child who he or she will turn to if someone is violating a rule or making them uncomfortable.

Try this exercise to help your child identify trusted adults.
Explain that a trusted adult is someone he or she knows well who is willing to listen and offer advice when needed. Trace your child's hand on a piece of paper. Ask your child to write or draw a person on each finger that he or she can go to for help or advice. Help your child determine the trusted adults. Explain that if a situation occurs where a trusted adult is needed, your child needs to remember this list. And if one of the people on the list cannot help, or is the one causing the problem, your child should go to another.

Ask your child these questions, making sure the options are understood (samples responses are given).

"What if something happens on a camping trip (or at a neighbor's house, or at a friend's house) that makes you feel afraid or confused?" I could talk to my pack leader about it right away. The pack leader said we could talk to them about anything that made us feel unsafe. When I get home, I would tell a parent what happened.

"What if someone is making you feel unsafe, and the first person you tell can't help you?" I would tell one of my other trusted grown-ups until I find one who can help.

"What if one of your trusted adults is making you feel unsafe or uncomfortable?" I am allowed to say NO to any adult who makes me feel afraid, confused, or unsafe. I would say NO and then contact one of the other adults on my list to get help.

Check First

Many abusers are known to the child as a family friend, relative, or older youth, so it is important to focus safety messages on the behavior of a person, not the relationship to the child. Teach your child to check with you first before agreeing to go anywhere with another person. Tell your child never to go anywhere with anyone who will not let him or her check with you first. If the person refuses, your child has the right to step back from the person, make noise, run away, and tell someone.

Tell your child that your permission is required before he or she may accept an invitation from a Scout leader or another parent to an activity outside of Scouting and that all such invitations must be reported to you. The BSA recommends that parents insist that two adults are present (two-deep leadership) when authorizing non-Scouting activities for their children.

Try this exercise to help your child remember to check first. Brainstorm times and situations in which your child should always come to you before going somewhere with someone. Include such situations as going into a house or vehicle, changing plans, being offered gifts, and being asked for help.

Talk through scenarios like the following.

"What if a neighbor asks you to come into his house to see his new puppy?" I would tell him that I need to check with you first. I would come home and check first before I went over to their house.

"What if you are playing in the park and a nice person asks you to come to a different part of the park to help him or her find something they lost?" I need to check first before changing my plans so that my parents know where I am. I also need to check first before helping an adult. Adults usually ask other adults for help. I can help if I check first and you come with me to ask my parents for permission.

Trust Your Gut Instinct—The "Uh-Oh" Feeling

Animals and humans have a gut instinct that helps keep us safe. Teach your child to listen to that "uh-oh" feeling that might occur if your child is in a place that does not feel right or with a person who is making him or her feel confused or scared. Encourage your child to go to a trusted adult if the "uh-oh" feeling starts.

Try this exercise to help your child learn to trust his or her gut instinct. Tell your child that any time someone makes his or her uh-oh feeling start, he or she has your permission to take some big steps back and say "NO," and then go tell a trusted adult what happened. Explain that stepping back can give him or her room to think and move. Then have your child practice taking big steps away from a person and saying "NO" in a firm voice.

Discuss the following situation with your child.

"What if someone drives up, gets out of their car, and starts walking toward you to ask you for directions?" My uh-oh alarm might go off, because I know adults should ask adults for help. I know I would need to check first. So I would start moving away from the person, say that I have to check first, and go quickly to the person taking care of me.

Secrets and Surprises

Sex offenders often try to groom children by convincing them to keep secrets about activities that they would not want their parents to know about (drinking, smoking, pornography, etc.). If the child wants to keep those activities secret, he or she might also see any abuse as something to keep secret. Your child must feel like he or she can come to you and be heard about little concerns as well as big problems. Tell your child it is not OK for people to ask him or her to keep a secret from you or another caregiver. Give your child a simple, automatic solution. Let your child know that he or she can come to you about anything and that you will still love and support him or her.

Try this exercise to help your child discern the difference between secrets and surprises. Tell your child that a secret is something that is hidden from others. A surprise is something that we keep quiet about for a short period of time and then everyone finds out together, like what you bought someone for his or her birthday. Surprises are usually OK, but secrets can be harmful if they cover up something unsafe or scary. Tell your child that if he or she is not sure that something is a secret or a surprise, he or she can always ask you or a trusted adult.

Ask your child what to do in the following situations.

"What if a bigger kid says he will give you $5 if you play a secret touching game with him?" My uh-oh alarm would probably go off, because that is against our family rules. I would take a few steps back, so I had room to think, and say NO in a strong voice. I would tell a trusted adult what happened.

"What if someone you know asks if he can email you a secret picture?" I would tell him that I don't want him to send it. If he sends it anyway, I would check with you first before opening the email. (For additional information, please see the BSA's Cyber Chip tool and resources at www.scouting.org/Training/YouthProtection/CyberChip.aspx and the NetSmartz Scouting Portal at www.netsmartz.org/scouting.)

Talk About Touches and Private Parts

Young people should be told that the parts of their body covered by their swimsuit are their private parts and they have the right to say no to being touched there. Body parts should be called by their appropriate names to assist in developing a healthy and positive body image. Encourage your child to say no and then tell you if someone tries to touch or look at his or her private parts or wants him or her to touch or look at their private parts.

It is important to remind children that if they get tricked into a scary or confusing touch or if they freeze and are unable to say no, it is OK and not their fault. Children should be encouraged to tell as soon as they feel comfortable doing so. Keep the lines of communication open by reminding them that they can talk to you about touches, even a long time after something happened.

Try this exercise to help your child resist someone who is trying to touch his or her private parts. Pose these scenarios with him or her, and then discuss the solutions.

"What if your friend's babysitter or another youth asks you to wrestle without clothes on?" I know that I am allowed to say NO to anyone asking me to do private part touches. I would take a few steps back so I have room to think, say NO in a strong voice, and head home.

"What if that same friend asks you to keep the touching games secret?" That would probably make my uh-oh alarm go off, because we don't keep secrets. I would let my friend know that what happened isn't his fault, and I would still come and tell you.

Putting It Together

Reviewing these five personal safety rules and allowing your child to design his or her own "What If" games can help make personal safety awareness less scary and more accessible for your child and the whole family. The most important points to make sure your child knows are as follows:

- Form a net.
- Check first.
- Trust your gut.
- Avoid secrets.
- Talk about touches.

Consider having a "Family Safety Night" at the beginning and the end of every school year or new activity. Reviewing rules about bike helmets, fire escape plans, and calling 911 should lead into conversations about personal safety awareness and online safety so that they can be treated like any other concern.

ADDITIONAL RESOURCES

The *Guide to Safe Scouting* exists to help members of the BSA conduct Scouting activities in a safe and prudent manner. It can be accessed online at www.scouting.org/health-and-safety/gss/.

Find your nearest BSA local council using the **Local Council Locator** at www.scouting.org/LocalCouncilLocator.aspx.

The **National Council's Youth Protection Team** can be contacted by email at Youth.Protection@scouting.org or by telephone at 972-580-2000.

BSA Youth Protection Materials

Along with this booklet, the Boy Scouts of America has an educational video for use by Cub Scout packs or dens. This award-winning production provides age-appropriate information about sexual abuse of children.

"It Happened to Me" is a video for Cub Scouts that portrays common situations in which sexual abuse can occur. The video discusses how sex offenders often resort to tricks for gaining access to their victims. It emphasizes that if children are sexually abused, they should talk to their parents or other trusted adults. The video also stresses that it is not the child's fault if he or she is sexually abused; it is the sex offender who is responsible. "It Happened to Me" is available from your BSA local council and should be shown to Cub Scouts 6 to 10 years of age only when a parent or other adult family member is present with the child. The BSA encourages the video to be viewed by each Cub Scout pack or den annually. Meeting guides in both English and Spanish can be found online at www.scouting.org/training/youthprotection/cubscout.aspx.

To help families and volunteers keep youth safe while online, the BSA introduced the **Cyber Chip** in conjunction with NetSmartz®. The material is tailored to each grade level for age-appropriateness. Go to www.scouting.org/cyberchip.

For Scouting's leaders and parents, the BSA has a video training session, **Youth Protection Guidelines: Training for Volunteer Leaders and Parents.** This is available from your BSA local council, with regular training sessions scheduled in most districts.

In addition to the video-based training, **Youth Protection training** is available on the BSA's website at www.scouting.org/Training/YouthProtection.aspx. The training addresses many questions Scouting volunteers and parents have regarding child sexual abuse.

In addition to these video and online materials, the BSA provides Youth Protection information to its members and families through **Boys' Life** and *Scouting* **magazines.**

For **more information** on Youth Protection, visit www.scouting.org/Training/YouthProtection.aspx.

Recommended Reading
Books for Children
My Body Belongs to Me by Jill Starishevsky (helping children learn about their bodies and assuring children that it is OK to tell)

It's My Body by Lory Freeman (teaching young children what to do about uncomfortable touches)

A Very Touching Book by Jan Hindman (teaching children what to do if there is "secret" touching; introduces and uses correct terms for genitals)

Books for Adults
How to Talk So Kids Will Listen & Listen So Kids Will Talk by Adele Faber and Elaine Mazlish (tested strategies to use for better parent/child communication)

Parents Preventing Abuse by Dr. Jaime Romo (e-book that guides parents to mitigate the conditions that allow child sexual abuse and prevent abuse of their children)

Protecting the Gift: Keeping Children and Teenagers Safe (and Parents Sane) by Gavin De Becker (how to help nurture your child's gut instinct as a protective factor)

Other Sources of Child Abuse Prevention Information
ChildHelp USA
4350 E. Camelback Road
Building F250
Phoenix, AZ 85018
National Child Abuse Hotline: 800-422-4453
www.childhelp.org

Child Welfare Information Gateway
1250 Maryland Ave. SW, 8th Floor
Washington, DC 20024
Telephone: 800-394-3366
info@childwelfare.gov
www.childwelfare.gov

National Suicide Prevention Lifeline
Telephone: 800-273-8255
www.suicidepreventionlifeline.org

National Center for Missing & Exploited Children
699 Prince St.
Alexandria, VA 22314-3175
Telephone: 800-843-5678 (CyberTipline)
www.missingkids.com
www.netsmartz.org

Prevent Child Abuse America
200 S. Wabash Ave., 10th Floor
Chicago, IL 60604
Telephone: 312-663-3520
www.preventchildabuse.org

stopbullying.gov
200 Independence Ave. SW
Washington, DC 20201

Acknowledgment

Special thanks to **Victor Vieth, J.D., Gundersen National Child Protection Training Center** for invaluable assistance in the development of this pamphlet.

Prepared. For Life.®

BOY SCOUTS OF AMERICA
1325 West Walnut Hill Lane
P.O. Box 152079
Irving, Texas 75015-2079
www.scouting.org

100-014
2018 Printing

WELCOME TO THE
WOLF
HANDBOOK

Being a Wolf Scout means enjoying awesome adventures.

Have a great year!

34752
ISBN 978-0-8395-0110-7
©2018 Boy Scouts of America
2018 Printing

Table of Contents

WOLF REQUIRED ADVENTURES

WOLF ELECTIVE ADVENTURES

Welcome, Wolf!

Welcome to a fun and exciting year of Cub Scouting, Wolf! You'll go on adventures, exploring the world around you with other Wolves in your den. You will play games, make fun things, learn about wildlife, and spend time outdoors. You'll even earn awards while having all this fun!

Note to Parents and Other Caring Adults

If you could give only one gift to the young people who are most important in your life, what would it be? No matter what your family situation is, it is within your power to help these children grow into people with a good feeling about themselves and a genuine concern for others. Cub Scouting can assist you in providing this greatest gift of all.

Most of the information in this book is written for the children who will participate, but we hope that you will look at it carefully and help your family to understand all that Cub Scouting has to offer. It would be great if you could read the adventures along with your Scout and help your Scout to enjoy the learning experience of achieving each adventure.

Every once in a while, you'll see a note for parents/adults in a box like this.

It's important to Scouting that every pack and den have great adult leadership. Packs are led by a Cubmaster and pack committee, while dens are guided by den leaders.

Parents help with den and pack activities and are encouraged to take training to prepare to become part of Cub Scout volunteer leadership. All adults who work directly with youth are required to take Youth Protection training.

Your Wolf Den

As a Wolf in the Boy Scouts of America, you belong to a den of kids who are Wolves just like you! They are in your grade or are the same age as you, and it will be fun to explore Wolf adventures with them at den meetings.

Your Cub Scout Pack

You, your family, and your den go to a monthly pack meeting, where everyone in all the dens in the pack get together at the same time. It's a chance to enjoy interesting programs and also a time for awards.

Cub Scouting and *The Jungle Book*

Great Britain's Lord Baden-Powell started worldwide Scouting in 1907, and the Boy Scouts of America began in 1910. Lord Baden-Powell really liked the stories in *The Jungle Book* by Rudyard Kipling. When Cub Scouting started in 1930, names and ideas were borrowed from *The Jungle Book* to make the program fun and exciting.

Lord Baden-Powell knew it was important to have a wise leader like Akela (Ah-KAY-la), the wolf. Akela lets the child Mowgli (MO-glee) join the wolf pack. Maybe you also know about Baloo the bear, who helps teach Mowgli the laws of the jungle so he can live among the animals.

To this day, we have names like Akela and Baloo and words like den and pack in Cub Scouting. That's our way of remembering how Cub Scouting began with *The Jungle Book*.

Wolf Leaders

In a real wolf pack in the wild, all the wolves look to their leader for guidance—when to work, when to learn, and when to play. A leader like Akela makes sure each young wolf learns about the world and how to get along with other members of the pack.

As a Wolf Scout, you have several people you can call Akela. These include the den leader, the assistant den leader, and your parent or guardian. Akela can be anyone who is older than you and is a wise teacher, just like Akela in *The Jungle Book*.

These leaders help you to learn new things, and they can even help you find new ways to use what you have already learned!

Did you know you can help lead your den by becoming a denner? The denner is a Scout chosen to help Akela at meetings and outings. If you're selected to be the denner, **do your best!**

"Do Your Best!" is the Cub Scout motto.

Your Wolf Uniform

Your uniform is an important part of being a Cub Scout. Wearing it lets people know that you belong to a Wolf den and a pack and, most important, you belong to the Boy Scouts of America! You should wear the uniform to den meetings, pack meetings, and any special activities you participate in as a Wolf.

The official uniform for Cub Scouts includes blue Cub Scout pants or shorts and shirt with insignia for your rank. Each rank has its own neckerchief and slide in the rank colors and a belt buckle to be worn with the blue Cub Scout belt. Wolf Scouts can also wear an official navy-blue cap with a red front panel and Wolf emblem.

Wearing the Cub Scout uniform shows you are a member of the team.

The pictures below show you where to put the Wolf Scout insignia on the sleeves and pockets of your uniform.

You might receive a patch for participating in day camp or a council popcorn sale. This is an example of "temporary insignia" and should be worn centered on the right pocket.

While serving as a denner, you will wear gold shoulder cords suspended from the left shoulder of your uniform.

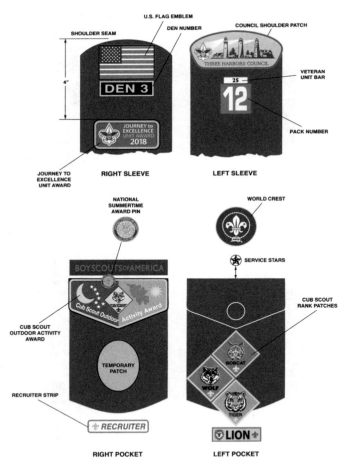

Wolf Adventures

The Cub Scout activities that you do with your den and family this year are called Wolf adventures. You'll have fun meeting the requirements with the help of your den leaders and other caring adults. Some of the adventures are ones that all Wolves will do, and others will be ones that you and your den choose.

When you have completed each required adventure and selected elective adventure, your den leader will give approval by signing your handbook. Once you have met all requirements, you will earn the rank of Wolf.

Note to Parents and Other Caring Adults

If your child is a new Cub Scout, the first step in the advancement process is to earn the Bobcat badge (see next chapter).

The Bobcat requirements introduce a new Scout to the ideals and symbols of Scouting. When all of the Bobcat requirements have been completed, your Scout becomes eligible to receive the Bobcat badge.

Character Compass

As you work on your Wolf adventures in the *Wolf Handbook*, you will notice this symbol:

A compass is a tool that guides a person from place to place. Character is how we act, and it guides our entire lives. This compass will be your guide to one or more of the 12 points of the Scout Law and will help you think about how the points of the Scout Law guide our way in Cub Scouting and in daily life. Those points are all different, and each one is a treasure for you to find.

THE OUTDOOR CODE

Much of Scouting, including Cub Scouting, happens outside. For more than 60 years, the Outdoor Code has been a guide for Scouts in the outdoors. Remember to do your best by showing respect for the outdoors and by learning and upholding the Outdoor Code.

THE OUTDOOR CODE

As an American, I will do my best to—

♦ Be clean in my outdoor manners,

♦ Be careful with fire,

♦ Be considerate in the outdoors, and

♦ Be conservation-minded.

Being clean in your outdoor manners, careful with fire, and considerate means you can enjoy the outdoors in ways that do no harm to the environment. Being conservation-minded encourages the protection and thoughtful use of natural resources and doing your part to improve the condition of the land and the environment.

As a Cub Scout, you will learn to use the Leave No Trace Principles for Kids to help you take care of an area where you hike or camp.

LEAVE NO TRACE PRINCIPLES FOR KIDS*

Center for Outdoor Ethics | LNT.org

1. Know Before You Go. Find out about the place you're going to camp ahead of time. Are there rules you need to know about? Are any activities against the rules? Is water available? Do you need to bring anything special?

2. Choose the Right Path. Always walk on trails, even if that means getting your boots muddy. Don't take shortcuts. Set up tents in marked camping areas.

3. Trash Your Trash. Use bathroom facilities when available. Follow campground rules for handling dishwater. Pack out all your trash unless the campground has trash pickup.

4. **Leave What You Find.** Leave any natural treasures where you find them so other campers can enjoy them, too. If you want a souvenir of your campout, take a picture. A good saying to remember is "Leave nothing but footprints, take nothing but pictures, kill nothing but time."

5. **Be Careful With Fire.** Cook on a camp stove or grill whenever possible. It's easier and less messy than cooking over an open fire. Only build fires in designated fire rings. Always have someone keep an eye on your fire until it is dead out.

6. **Respect Wildlife.** Travel quietly and give animals enough space that you don't disturb them. Getting too close to an animal can potentially hurt the animal and you. Take pictures from a safe distance. You're visiting the animal's home, so be considerate.

7. **Be Kind to Other Visitors.** Be respectful of other visitors by keeping noise down and not entering other groups' campsites without permission. Be polite to other people you meet. Give them the respect you expect from them.

To help you remember the Outdoor Code and the Leave No Trace Principles for Kids, you can find them in the back of your handbook.

The member-driven Leave No Trace Center for Outdoor Ethics teaches people how to enjoy the outdoors responsibly. This copyrighted information has been reprinted with permission from the Leave No Trace Center for Outdoor Ethics: www.LNT.org.

Bobcat!

If you haven't already earned your Bobcat badge, you will start your Cub Scouting adventures by learning what it means to become a Scout.

Read through the Bobcat requirements and practice several times what you have learned. When you think that you are ready, share what you've learned with your family and your den leader. Then give yourself a pat on the back and congratulate yourself on earning your Bobcat badge.

BOBCAT REQUIREMENTS

1. Learn and say the Scout Oath, with help if needed.
2. Learn and say the Scout Law, with help if needed.
3. Show the Cub Scout sign. Tell what it means.
4. Show the Cub Scout handshake. Tell what it means.
5. Say the Cub Scout motto. Tell what it means.
6. Show the Cub Scout salute. Tell what it means.
7. With your parent or guardian, complete the exercises in the pamphlet *How to Protect Your Children From Child Abuse: A Parent's Guide.*

One of the most important parts of earning Bobcat is understanding that all Scouts believe in and work to live by the Scout Oath and the Scout Law. We learn those words and believe in them as a way to live our lives and be good members of our families, our communities, and the Cub Scout pack.

Scout Oath

On my honor I will do my best
To do my duty to God and my country
and to obey the Scout Law;
To help other people at all times;
To keep myself physically strong,
mentally awake, and morally straight.

The Meaning of the Scout Oath

ON MY HONOR ...

Saying "On my honor" is like saying "I promise."

I WILL DO MY BEST ...

This means that you will do your best to do what the Scout Oath says.

The Scout Oath has several parts.
Let's look at what they mean.

TO DO MY DUTY ... A duty is something you are expected to do. At home, you might be expected to make up your bed or take out the trash. You also have duties to God and to your country.

TO GOD ... You do your duty to God by following the teachings of your family and religious leaders.

AND MY COUNTRY ... You do your duty to your country by being a good citizen and obeying the law.

AND TO OBEY THE SCOUT LAW; ... You also promise to live by the 12 points of the Scout Law, which are described on the next page.

TO HELP OTHER PEOPLE AT ALL TIMES; ... Many people need help. A friendly smile and a helping hand make life easier for others. By helping other people, you are doing a Good Turn and making our world a better place.

TO KEEP MYSELF PHYSICALLY STRONG, ... This part of the Scout Oath is about taking care of yourself. You stay physically strong when you eat the right foods and get plenty of exercise.

MENTALLY AWAKE, ... You stay mentally awake when you work hard in school, learn all you can, and ask questions.

AND MORALLY STRAIGHT. You stay morally straight when you do the right thing and live your life with honesty.

Date   Den Leader's OK

Scout Law

A Scout is trustworthy, loyal, helpful, friendly, courteous, kind, obedient, cheerful, thrifty, brave, clean, and reverent.

The Meaning of the Scout Law

The Scout Law has 12 points. Each is a goal for every Scout. A Scout tries to live up to the Law every day. It is not always easy to do, but a Scout always tries.

A Scout is TRUSTWORTHY. Tell the truth and keep your promises. People can depend on you.

A Scout is LOYAL. Be true to your family, friends, Scout leaders, school, and country.

A Scout is HELPFUL. Volunteer to help others without expecting a reward.

A Scout is FRIENDLY. Be a friend to everyone, even people who are very different from you.

A Scout is COURTEOUS. Be polite to everyone and always use good manners.

A Scout is KIND. Treat others as you want to be treated. Never harm or kill any living thing without good reason.

A Scout is OBEDIENT. Follow the rules of your family, school, and pack. Obey the laws of your community and country.

A Scout is CHEERFUL. Look for the bright side of life. Cheerfully do tasks that come your way. Try to help others be happy.

A Scout is THRIFTY. Work to pay your own way. Don't be wasteful. Use time, property, and natural resources wisely.

A Scout is BRAVE. Face difficult situations even when you feel afraid. Do what is right despite what others might be doing or saying.

A Scout is CLEAN. Keep your body and mind fit. Help keep your home and community clean.

A Scout is REVERENT. Be reverent toward God. Be faithful in your religious duties. Respect the beliefs of others.

_____   _____
Date   Den Leader's OK

Make the sign with your right hand. Hold your arm straight up. The two raised fingers stand for the Scout Oath and the Scout Law. The fingers look like the sharp ears of the wolf ready to listen to Akela! Remember that Akela means "good leader" to a Cub Scout. Your mother or father or guardian is Akela. So is your Cubmaster or your den leader. At school, your teacher is Akela.

3

Date   Den Leader's OK

When you shake hands with another Cub Scout, do this: Hold out your right hand just as you always do to shake hands. But then put your first two fingers along the inside of the other Scout's wrist. This means that you help each other to remember and obey the Scout Oath and Scout Law.

4

Date   Den Leader's OK

The Cub Scout motto is "Do Your Best."

A motto is a guiding principle and a rule for living. Do Your Best means trying your hardest, not just a little bit. Do your best all the time. Do your best in school and at home. Do your best when you play a game and help your team. Do your best as you work on your rank adventures!

_____   _____
Date   **Den Leader's OK**

6 | **Show the Cub Scout salute. Tell what it means.**

Salute with your right hand. Hold your first two fingers close together. Touch your fingertips to your cap. If you aren't wearing a cap, touch your right eyebrow.

Salute the flag to show respect to our country. Always use the Cub Scout salute when you are in your Cub Scout uniform, both indoors

and outdoors. If you are not in uniform, you salute the flag by placing your right hand over your heart.

Date   Den Leader's OK

7 | **With your parent or guardian, complete the exercises in the pamphlet How to Protect Your Children From Child Abuse: A Parent's Guide.**

If your handbook does not include the pamphlet, talk with your den leader.

Date   Den Leader's OK

Congratulations on earning your Bobcat badge! You may now continue on the trail of your Wolf adventures. Let's take a look at what those adventures are called, what you need to do to earn your Wolf badge, and all the fun things you will explore as a Wolf.

The Wolf Adventures and Requirements

WOLF BADGE REQUIREMENTS

Note to Parents and Other Caring Adults

Requirements do not need to be completed in any particular order. In developing the plan for the order in which to do the Wolf adventures, den leaders will look at many factors, including seasonal considerations. Note that both Paws on the Path and Call of the Wild include activities to be done in the out-of-doors.

1. Complete each of the six required adventures.

 *Call of the Wild

 Howling at the Moon

 Council Fire (Duty to Country)

 *Paws on the Path

 Duty to God Footsteps

 Running With the Pack

*Seasonal considerations

2. In addition to the six required adventures listed previously, complete at least one elective adventure of your den's or family's choosing.

WOLF ELECTIVE ADVENTURES

 Adventures in Coins

 Germs Alive!

 Air of the Wolf

 Grow Something

 Code of the Wolf

 Hometown Heroes

 Collections and Hobbies

 Motor Away

 Cubs Who Care

 Paws of Skill

 Digging in the Past

 Spirit of the Water

 Finding Your Way

3. With your parent, guardian, or other caring adult, complete the exercises in the pamphlet *How to Protect Your Children From Child Abuse: A Parent's Guide.*

4. Earn the Cyber Chip award for your age. (The Cyber Chip portion of this requirement may be waived by your parent or guardian if you do not have access to the internet.)

Once you have achieved all of the Wolf rank badge requirements and your handbook has been signed, you are ready to earn your Wolf badge!

Let out a big GRAND HOWL, Wolf Scout!

CALL OF THE WILD

REQUIRED ADVENTURE

Complete requirements 1-4 plus at least one other.

1. Attend one of the following:

    A. A pack or family campout

    B. An outdoor activity with your den or pack

    C. Day camp

    D. Resident camp

2. With your family or den, make a list of possible weather changes that could happen during your outing according to the time of year you are outside. Tell how you will be prepared for each one.

3. Do the following:

    A. Recite the Outdoor Code with your leader.

    B. Recite the Leave No Trace Principles for Kids with your leader. Talk about how these principles support the Outdoor Code.

    C. After your outdoor activity or campout, list the ways you demonstrated being careful with fire or other dangers.

4. Show or demonstrate what to do:

    A. In case of a natural disaster such as an earthquake or flood.

    B. To keep from spreading your germs.

5. Show how to tie an overhand knot and a square knot.

6. While on a den or family outing, identify four different types of animals you see or explain evidence of their presence. Tell how you identified them.

SNAPSHOT OF ADVENTURE

You are about to have an adventure in the outdoors. Before you go, plan what you need to bring. Your den leader or another caring adult will help you get ready.

Each time you go camping or to another outdoor activity, you can show you are a Wolf Scout by doing more on your own. Learn more about the animals you may see, how to tie a few basic knots, how to prepare for the weather, and how to handle different outdoor situations. Let's go, Wolf!

COMPLETE REQUIREMENTS 1–4 PLUS AT LEAST ONE OTHER.

REQUIREMENT 1 | Attend one of the following:

REQUIREMENT 1A | A pack or family campout

REQUIREMENT 1B | An outdoor activity with your den or pack

REQUIREMENT 1C | Day camp

REQUIREMENT 1D | Resident camp

Telling stories, toasting marshmallows, looking at the stars, sleeping in a tent—these are just a few of the activities waiting for you, depending on the camping or outing.

But before you go, what should you bring?

Start with the Cub Scout Six Essentials:

Trail food

Filled water bottle

First-aid kit, including adhesive bandages, antibiotic ointment, and other items

Whistle

Sun protection

Flashlight (check the batteries)

Now, make a complete list of what you need to bring. The list on the next page includes items you might want on a family or pack campout. Discuss with your pack or your family which items are needed.

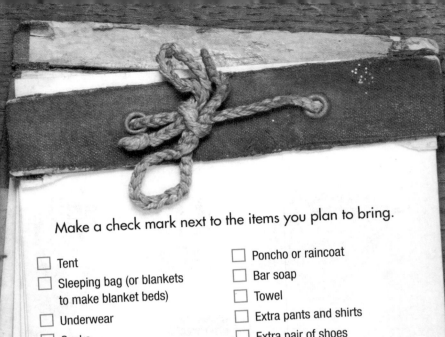

Make a check mark next to the items you plan to bring.

- ☐ Tent
- ☐ Sleeping bag (or blankets to make blanket beds)
- ☐ Underwear
- ☐ Socks
- ☐ Pajamas
- ☐ Knife, fork, spoon
- ☐ Plates, bowls, cups
- ☐ Trash bag
- ☐ Insect repellent
- ☐ Toothbrush and toothpaste
- ☐ Toilet paper
- ☐ Sweater or jacket

- ☐ Poncho or raincoat
- ☐ Bar soap
- ☐ Towel
- ☐ Extra pants and shirts
- ☐ Extra pair of shoes
- ☐ *Wolf Handbook*
- ☐ Bible, testament, prayer book, or other book for your faith

GROUP EQUIPMENT CAN INCLUDE:

- ☐ Cooking pot or pan
- ☐ Pliers
- ☐ Plastic sheet for air-drying dishes
- ☐ Camp stove or charcoal
- ☐ Food for all camp meals
- ☐ A cooler to keep perishable foods cold
- ☐ Waterproof groundsheets
- ☐ Hammer for stakes

When you go camping for the first time, you can often use borrowed or substitute equipment. For many Scouts, their first mess kit is a plastic bowl that used to hold whipped dessert topping. As you go camping more often, you can add to your equipment.

Before you leave on your outing, check off the list to make sure you have everything. Make sure your gear works and you have everything you need to set up.

When you return, talk with your den or family about the fun you had and how prepared you felt with the gear that you took.

_____   _____
Date   Den Leader's OK

Camping is great when you are ready for any kind of weather. If you get caught in a rain shower in a T-shirt, you will be sopping wet and cold. But if you have rubber boots and a waterproof jacket and pants, you can keep on having fun!

With your den leader or parent, talk about the different kinds of weather that could happen where you are going to camp or while you are on an outing. Can the temperature or weather change a lot from morning to night? Make a list below of possible weather you could run into. Write the gear you will bring along to be prepared for the weather.

Weather	What I will bring to be prepared
_____	_____
_____	_____
_____	_____

_____   _____
Date   **Den Leader's OK**

REQUIREMENT 3 | Do the following:

REQUIREMENT 3A | Recite the Outdoor Code with your leader.

As a Scout, it is your job to help leave any park or camping area better than the way you found it. Learn the Outdoor Code so you'll be ready.

OUTDOOR CODE

As an American, I will do my best to—

- Be clean in my outdoor manners,
- Be careful with fire,
- Be considerate in the outdoors, and
- Be conservation-minded.

One part of the Outdoor Code is a promise to be careful with fire. When you are safe with fire, you are being clean in your outdoor manners, considerate in the outdoors, and conservation-minded.

CAMPFIRE SAFETY

Always have adult supervision for campfires. Only build fires in designated or approved places. This may be an area that is on the ground or a raised fire pit that is far away from trees and brush.

Put out every fire when you no longer need it. Make sure it is completely out. The ground where the fire was burning should be cold. Clean up the campfire site and return any materials you moved to their original places. The site should look just as it did when you arrived.

CAMP STOVE SAFETY

Sometimes a camp stove will be used for cooking. There are also rules to keep you safe around a camp stove.

1. Only cook on a camp stove with help from an adult.

2. An adult must always fill and light the stove.

3. Avoid wearing loose or baggy clothing and tie back long hair when you are cooking.

3A _____   _____
          Date   **Den Leader's OK**

REQUIREMENT 3B | Recite the Leave No Trace Principles for Kids with your leader. Talk about how these principles support the Outdoor Code.

The principles of Leave No Trace help Scouts and others enjoy time in nature without causing harm to it. There are seven Leave No Trace Principles for Kids, and they share many of the same goals as the Outdoor Code.

LEAVE NO TRACE* PRINCIPLES FOR KIDS

- ◆ Know Before You Go
- ◆ Choose the Right Path
- ◆ Trash Your Trash
- ◆ Leave What You Find
- ◆ Be Careful With Fire
- ◆ Respect Wildlife
- ◆ Be Kind to Other Visitors

*The member-driven Leave No Trace Center for Outdoor Ethics teaches people how to enjoy the outdoors responsibly. This copyrighted information has been reprinted with permission from the Leave No Trace Center for Outdoor Ethics: www.LNT.org.

Can you see how these principles will help you live out the Outdoor Code? With your den leader, discuss ways that you will demonstrate the principle "Be Careful With Fire" on your campout.

_____   _____
Date   **Den Leader's OK**

REQUIREMENT 3C | **After your outdoor activity or campout, list the ways you demonstrated being careful with fire or other dangers.**

Think about the times you were near the campfire or a stove on your campout. What other dangers did you identify and avoid? Explain to your den leader how you followed the Outdoor Code and the Leave No Trace Principles for Kids by being careful with fire. In the space below, write what you did.

I was careful with fire and avoided other dangers when I ...

_____

_____

_____   _____
Date   **Den Leader's OK**

REQUIREMENT 4 | Show or demonstrate what to do:

REQUIREMENT 4A | In case of a natural disaster such as an earthquake or flood.

Being prepared also means knowing how to keep yourself safe and healthy. Here are some ways to prevent danger, injury, and sickness in the outdoors.

NATURAL DISASTERS

Ask your den leader or someone in your family what types of natural disasters have happened where you live. Talk about what you can do to be prepared. If a disaster ever happens, what can you do to protect yourself?

In any natural disaster, staying calm will help you stay safe.

Each type of natural disaster may also call for certain actions. For example, if you are camping near a river or creek and it floods, you may have only moments to run to higher ground.

Put a check mark beside the disasters that could happen near you. In the space to the right, write down one thing you can do to stay safe if this kind of disaster happens.

Natural Disaster	One thing I can do to stay safe
☐ Flood	_____
☐ Earthquake	_____
☐ Wildfire	_____
☐ Blizzard	_____
☐ Hurricane	_____
☐ Tornado	_____

4A

_____   _____
Date   **Den Leader's OK**

THE BEST WAY TO STAY WELL?
WASH YOUR HANDS!

It isn't fun to be sick on a campout! The best way to stay healthy and to keep from spreading germs is to wash your hands often with soap and water. This is true no matter where you are. Follow these steps to show you know the proper way to wash your hands. Always wash your hands after you use the restroom and before you eat or you help cook a meal.

Use soap.

Rub for 20 seconds.

Rinse.

Dry with a towel,
and then turn off the
faucet with a towel.

A Scout is courteous. When you wash your hands, you are being polite to others around you.

_____   _____
Date   **Den Leader's OK**

Tying knots is an important Scout skill. It is also something you will use throughout your life. Some of the knots you will learn in Scouting have been used for thousands of years.

Every knot has a special purpose. Some knots join pieces of rope together. Some knots that don't slip are used for rescues. Other knots are perfect for tying down equipment—you can adjust these knots and they will still hold.

You will learn how to tie knots to do specific things. All correctly tied knots can be easily untied.

OVERHAND KNOT

An overhand knot is simple. You can use it to keep a rope from going through a pulley or a hole, or to make a rope easier to grip.

An overhand knot is also the first step for some other knots. You will need a single strand of rope to practice this knot.

1. First, make a loop in the end of a rope.

2. Next, tuck the end of the rope through the loop.

3. Pull the end of the rope to tighten the knot.

Hint: Do you need a larger knot to stop a rope from going through a big hole? You can make a larger stopper knot by adding a second overhand knot after the first one.

SQUARE KNOT

The main use of a square knot is to join the ends of two ropes. This is why it is called the joining knot in Scouting.

You can use both ends of one piece of rope to make a square knot or two different pieces of rope.

1. Hold one end of a rope in one hand and the other end of the rope in your other hand.

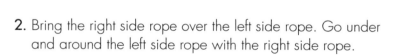

2. Bring the right side rope over the left side rope. Go under and around the left side rope with the right side rope.

3. Now bring the left side rope over the right side rope. Go under and around the right side rope with the left side rope.

4. Pull both ends firmly. The knot will not hold its shape without being tightened.

The square knot is simply right over left, left over right.

You can use a square knot to tie bundles together. You also use the first half of a square knot when you tie your shoelaces.

Remember, the square knot is not to be trusted when safety is important. Just like your shoelaces, a square knot can sometimes come undone.

@ You can find more cool knots to master (with a parent's permission) at **boyslife.org/video-audio/644/learn-to-tie-knots/** or in books at **www.scoutstuff.org.**

Scouts who know their knots and when to use them will be a great help on Scouting adventures!

Date   Den Leader's OK

When you are outdoors, you share the area with animals that live there. They may be birds, mammals, insects, reptiles, or other creatures. Knowing the animals that live in an area is a way for Wolf Scouts to be prepared. For example, when you are camping in some parks and wilderness areas, you may have to use a bear bag or take other steps to keep your food safe from animals.

Learning more about the animals that live near you is also an important outdoor skill. The more you know, the more connected you will feel to the place where you live and the natural world around you.

Instead of saying, "I saw a butterfly," you can say, "I saw a monarch butterfly with orange and black wings." In learning to identify a monarch butterfly, you might also learn that monarchs, like many birds, fly south in the fall and north in the spring. In fact, monarchs can migrate more than 2,500 miles a year!

Your den leader or another adult will help you learn about the animals that live nearby. Make a list below. Write down how you can identify each animal.

Animal	How I can identify it
1. _____	_____
	_____
2. _____	_____
	_____
3. _____	_____
	_____
4. _____	_____
	_____

6

_____   _____
Date   **Den Leader's OK**

My Camping/Outdoor Activity Experience

_____

_____

_____

_____

_____

_____

_____

_____

_____

_____

_____

_____

_____

_____

_____

COUNCIL FIRE
(DUTY TO COUNTRY)

REQUIRED ADVENTURE

Complete requirements 1 and 2 plus at least one other.

1. With your den or pack, participate in a flag ceremony, and learn how to properly care for and fold the flag.

2. Participate in a community service project with your pack, den, or family.

3. With your parent's or guardian's permission, talk to a military veteran, law enforcement officer, member of the fire department, or someone else approved by your den leader. Talk about his or her service to the community or country. After you have visited with the individual, write a short thank-you note.

4. Learn about the changes in your community, and create a project to show your den how the community has changed.

5. Select one issue in your community, and present to your den your ideas for a solution to the problem.

6. Work with your den to develop a den duty chart, and perform these tasks for one month.

7. Participate in an event such as a parade or assembly celebrating military veterans.

SNAPSHOT OF ADVENTURE

A real wolf pack works like a large family where everyone works together to keep the members of the pack safe, healthy, and happy. Working together is part of being a good citizen. In this adventure, you will be a part of different groups—your den, your pack, your family, and your community.

I pledge allegiance to the Flag of the United States of America, and to the Republic for which it stands, one Nation under God, indivisible, with liberty and justice for all.

REQUIREMENT 1 | With your den or pack, participate in a flag ceremony, and learn how to properly care for and fold the flag.

Learning how to show respect for the flag and how to care for it are parts of being a good citizen.

One way American citizens show respect is by having a flag ceremony. Your leader will show you the steps of the ceremony and the proper way to fold the flag.

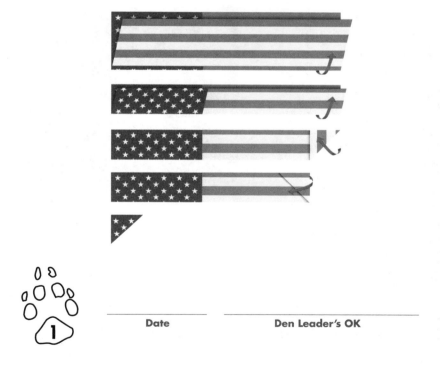

Date

Den Leader's OK

You and your Wolf den will feel great when you work together to make your community a better place!

A Scout is loyal. When you work with your den on a community service project, you are showing that you are loyal to your community.

An important part of the Scout Law is "To help other people at all times." Service projects are one way Cub Scouts help other people and their community. You, your den, and Akela can decide on the type of service project you want to accomplish. Here are some ideas for community service projects:

- ◆ Plant a tree (or two or three) that is native to your area.

- ◆ Clean up a vacant lot, or paint over graffiti on a wall.

- ◆ Plant and care for flowers that are native to your area in a public place.

- ◆ Volunteer your den's time to help out at a food bank or host a food drive.

- ◆ Improve a trail, or clean up along the banks of a local creek.

- Visit a senior center and talk with residents as you deliver cards or plants or help in some other way.
- Help your chartered organization by performing yardwork.

A good service project takes planning with your den to make it a big success. You and your den should bring along any supplies needed to complete your service project. Be sure to get permission in advance from those in charge of the location before you start. You and your Wolf den will feel great when you work together to make your community a better place while helping others at the same time.

_____   _____
Date   **Den Leader's OK**

In the wild, adult wolves in a pack work together to protect the whole pack from danger. Men and women keep our communities and our country safe by serving as law enforcement officers, emergency care providers, firefighters, and military service members.

When you meet with a first responder, community worker, or military veteran from your area, shake hands and thank the person for his or her service. Ask about the reasons he or she became a public servant or volunteered to serve in the military. Find out more about the work he or she does to improve the community or keep us safe here at home.

After you meet with a public servant or military veteran, write and send a thank-you note. Say thank-you for taking the time to meet with you. Be sure to express your appreciation to the person for his or her service.

_____   _____
Date   Den Leader's OK

REQUIREMENT 4 | Learn about the changes in your community, and create a project to show your den how the community has changed.

How would you describe the community where you live? Is it a big city, a small town, or a suburb, or in a rural area?

Have you ever looked around your community and noticed that something is different? Maybe an empty lot is now a playground. Or maybe a new school was built in a place that was once a field. Towns and cities are changing all the time. And there is a good chance that your community looks very different from the way it looked many years ago.

Salt Lake City between 1870 and 1890

Salt Lake City, 1904   Salt Lake City, present day

Look for pictures and stories about your community when it was first settled or early in its history. Perhaps you can find old postcards that show how your town looked long ago.

You might be able to take a picture of the same location now to show how it has changed! Or look for photos of your town that have been taken recently. With the help of your parent or another caring adult, you can find a lot of interesting facts and pictures about your community at your local library.

Create a project to show how your town has changed, and share it with your den. Discuss with your den how your community has changed over time.

_____   _____
Date   **Den Leader's OK**

Every community has to deal with issues—important subjects or problems that people talk about to decide what to do. Sometimes, people have very different views on what should be done. With the help of your parent or another caring adult, use local news from TV, newspapers, or the internet to learn about issues in your community.

For example, if you live in an area that is growing a lot but has experienced a long drought, one issue may be the water supply. What does your town plan to do so that everyone in the future has enough water? Does your community encourage people to conserve water? What are some key ideas of the plan and how will they help?

Maybe your town has a lot of old buildings that are empty and in need of repair. Do some people want to repair them, but others want to tear them down and build bigger, modern buildings?

Now think about the issue yourself. What do you think should happen? Why? When you meet with your den, share your ideas for solving this issue with your den leader. Listen quietly to everyone's ideas. Are there different ways to solve the problem? Can you see why people must work together toward a common goal to solve community issues?

🗒 **TOWN NEWS** ★★★
Community Center Plans
A town meeting will be held next week to discuss

_____   _____
Date   **Den Leader's OK**

Like any team, your Wolf den has to work together to get things done. Chores get completed faster and are more fun when you're working with your Wolf buddies.

With your den leader, make a list of the things that have to be done every week before and after your den meeting.

Do you move tables and chairs together that must be put back after your meeting? Do you need to clean up after your meeting? Did you work on a craft or have food and drinks? Do you have den supplies to take care of?

Work with your den to figure out a duty list. Your den leader will give each den member a job to do from this list. Each Wolf will have a job to do for the next month. Pitch in and be cheerful! Remember to finish your duty each time you meet.

Date	Den Leader's OK

Honoring and showing respect for our country's military veterans is one way we can express our gratitude for the service they have provided to our country.

Participating in a parade or assembly that celebrates our veterans is both educational and fun.

As you plan how you will participate, think about how you will dress (probably in uniform), whether and how you will carry flags, and how you will prepare for your part in any ceremony.

With your den, talk about what it means to show respect at this type of event.

Date	Den Leader's OK

DUTY TO GOD FOOTSTEPS

REQUIRED ADVENTURE

Complete requirement 1 or 2 plus at least two others.

1. Discuss with your parent, guardian, den leader, or other caring adult what it means to do your duty to God. Tell how you do your duty to God in your daily life.

2. Earn the religious emblem of your faith that is appropriate for your age, if you have not already done so.

3. Offer a prayer, meditation, or reflection with your family, den, or pack.

4. Read a story about people or groups of people who came to America to enjoy religious freedom.

5. Learn and sing a song that could be sung in reverence before or after meals or one that gives encouragement, reminds you how to show reverence, or demonstrates your duty to God.

6. Visit a religious monument or site where people might show reverence. Create a visual display of your visit with your den or your family, and show how it made you feel reverent or helped you better understand your duty to God.

SNAPSHOT OF ADVENTURE

Duty to God is part of the Scout Oath, and being reverent is the 12th point of the Scout Law. In Scouting, you are encouraged to learn more about your own faith and to respect the faith of others. In this adventure, you will complete most of these requirements with your family and/or your religious leaders. Faith means having complete trust or confidence in someone or something. Always be respectful when talking about your faith and when learning about other faiths.

Note to Parents and Other Caring Adults

Inspiration and support for your child's spiritual development will come primarily from your family and/or faith leaders. While reverence and duty to God have always been part of Scouting values, the Boy Scouts of America does not promote any specific religion and is completely nonsectarian. There is no requirement that Scouts identify with a particular religion or faith.

In keeping with these principles, your Scout will need your guidance to complete requirements for this Duty to God Footsteps adventure. Please let the den leader know when your Scout has completed each requirement.

COMPLETE REQUIREMENT 1 OR 2 PLUS AT LEAST TWO OTHERS.

REQUIREMENT 1 | Discuss with your parent, guardian, den leader, or other caring adult what it means to do your duty to God. Tell how you do your duty to God in your daily life.

Having faith in God is an important part of being a good Cub Scout. Following the traditions, customs, and teachings of your faith is how you show reverence. How you act and treat other people is another way you can put your faith into practice.

There are many ways that different religions show their reverence to God. Sharing your faith with your family creates a special bond. Discuss your faith with your family. What does your faith say about how you treat others?

Many faiths and societies have a common and simple rule. Over time this has come to be known as the Golden Rule: "Do unto others as you would have done unto you." It simply means don't do something to someone if you wouldn't want them to

do it to you. For example, if you like to be treated with kindness and respect, you should treat others the same way.

A Scout is kind. Showing kindness to others is one way many people demonstrate their duty to God.

REQUIREMENT 2 | Earn the religious emblem of your faith that is appropriate for your age, if you have not already done so.

To encourage members to grow stronger in their faith, religious groups have developed and administer religious emblems programs for different grade levels. The Boy Scouts of America has approved these programs and allows emblems to be worn on the official uniform. For more information about the Religious Emblems Program, visit www.scouting.org/Awards/ReligiousAwards.aspx.

REQUIREMENT 3 | Offer a prayer, meditation, or reflection with your family, den, or pack.

In Scouting, we use prayers to show reverence. We show our respect for God when we pause and offer thanks for the things we have in our lives, such as family and good health. Scouts should follow the guidelines of their family's faith when they pray and be respectful of how other Scouts show their faith.

Different faiths have different customs when they pray. For example, some might wear special head coverings, raise or cross their arms, or kneel on special rugs when they pray. Prayers that are not specific to any one religion are called nondenominational.

One well-known nondenominational prayer in Scouting is called the Philmont Grace, which is said before meals at Philmont Scout Ranch in New Mexico. Scouts who visit Philmont learn the prayer and share it with their fellow Scouts and families when they return home.

Philmont Grace

For food, for raiment,

For life, for opportunity,

For friendship and fellowship,

We thank thee, O Lord. Amen.

For this requirement, you can make up your own simple prayer to say with your family, den, or pack. You can also find interfaith prayers in the BSA pamphlet "A Scout Is Reverent," found at www.scouting.org/filestore/pdf/interfaithservice.pdf. Have your parent or guardian help you select some that support your family's beliefs.

Here are some examples of interfaith prayers:

- For health, strength, and daily food, we give you thanks, O God.
- For this and all your mercies, God, make us truly grateful.
- For food, health, and friendship, we give you thanks, O God.

Date	Den Leader's OK

Note to Parents and Other Caring Adults

Please let your Scout's den leader know when this requirement has been completed.

REQUIREMENT 4 | Read a story about people or groups of people who came to America to enjoy religious freedom.

Many people overcame great difficulties to come to America so they could be free to practice their religions. In fact, many of the first 13 colonies were formed by people who had been persecuted, or treated badly, in their home countries in Europe because of their faiths. From the earliest days in our country's history, American citizens demanded that their personal freedoms be protected, including their right to practice their religion. The First Amendment to the U.S. Constitution does just that! In addition to protecting our freedom of speech, press, assembly, and petition, it protects Americans' rights to practice their religions.

William Penn

America is a place for people from different backgrounds and many faiths. You may want to read about the Pilgrims, who came to America from Europe about 400 years ago, or look for stories about modern-day people who came here seeking religious freedom.

With help from your parent or guardian, find and read a story about people who came to this country seeking religious freedom. Talk with your family about what you learned.

_____   _____
Date   Den Leader's OK

REQUIREMENT 5 | Learn and sing a song that could be sung in reverence before or after meals or one that gives encouragement, reminds you how to show reverence, or demonstrates your duty to God.

Choose a song that shows reverence or duty to God. It might be a song you can sing as a grace before meals, one that encourages someone, or a morning song to help you prepare for the day ahead. It might also be an evening song to help you thank God for all that happened that day. You can find many songs of faith in the *Cub Scout Songbook*.

With your family or den, sing the song you selected.

_____   _____
Date   Den Leader's OK

64 ▪ Wolf

REQUIREMENT 6 | **Visit a religious monument or site where people might show reverence. Create a visual display of your visit with your den or your family, and show how it made you feel reverent or helped you better understand your duty to God.**

Many people throughout America's history have placed their faith in God. In good times and in bad, in times of war and peace, they believed that God would see them through the challenges they faced.

Gettysburg Cemetery

There are many religious monuments and historic sites that honor people for their service. While some mark great battles and terrible sacrifices made by Americans, others are the sacred places of people who have always called America home. Some sites are places of worship where people gather to pray and reflect on their faith. At such sites, we can learn more about people of faith and remember them with respect and reverence. These sites also help us think about the footprints these people left in their journeys through life.

Now it is your turn to visit a religious monument or historic site near where you live. Take photos or draw some pictures. With your den or your family, put together a visual display that tells the story of your trip. What impressed you about the place you visited or the person or people honored there? Show how the visit made you feel reverent or strengthened your faith in God.

Robert Baden-Powell started Boy Scouts in England more than 100 years ago. He taught Scouts to be reverent toward God, to respect each other's religion, and to treat each other like brothers.

"Every Scout should have a religion," he said. "Religion seems a very simple thing: First: Love and serve God. Second: Love and serve your neighbor."

There is a museum about Baden-Powell's life at the National Scouting Museum at Philmont Scout Ranch in Cimarron, New Mexico. Scouts who visit the museum can learn about Baden-Powell as the founder of Scouting.

Cub Scout families can go to the Philmont Training Center, where adults can attend training and Cub Scouts and other family members can participate in fun and unique activities.

A Scout is reverent. Visiting places that honor people of faith is one way to show reverence.

6

_____ _____
Date   **Den Leader's OK**

Note to Parents and Other Caring Adults

Please let your Scout's den leader know when this requirement has been completed.

HOWLING AT THE MOON

REQUIRED ADVENTURE

Complete the following requirements.

1. Show you can communicate in at least two different ways.
2. Work with your den or family to create an original skit.
3. Work together with your den or family to plan, prepare, and rehearse a campfire program to present at a den meeting or pack program.
4. Perform your role for a den meeting or pack program.

SNAPSHOT OF ADVENTURE

For many years, people believed that wolves howl at the moon. Wolves actually howl to communicate with one another. For example, a wolf might howl to mean, "I want to meet up with the pack," or "Here's where I am." During this adventure, you will get a chance to do your own howling. You will show you can communicate in different ways, create and perform a skit, and help put on a Wolf show.

REQUIREMENT 1 | Show you can communicate in at least two different ways.

How can you make someone who does not speak your language understand you? Can you act out a story without speaking? Can you draw a picture?

There are four different ways to communicate:
1. Verbal communication is when you use your voice to communicate, like when you talk or sing.
2. Non-verbal communication uses facial expression, body language, and motions to communicate without words.
3. Written communication is just that. People write in letters, emails, books, magazines, newspapers, and material on the internet.
4. Visual communication includes graphs, charts, maps, photographs, and art to tell stories.

   How many of these ways do you use to communicate?

People who are deaf or hard of hearing cannot hear what others say. Many speak using another type of language called American Sign Language (ASL). You can learn the Cub Scout motto in American Sign Language.

Cub Scout

Motto

Do

Your

Best

A Scout is helpful. If someone is having difficulty communicating, be helpful by listening carefully and patiently. Remember, not being understood can be frustrating.

_____   _____
Date   **Den Leader's OK**

REQUIREMENT 2 | Work with your den or family to create an original skit.

Get ready to communicate "fun"! Create an original skit with your den or family. Skit ideas can come from your imagination, jokes from books or *Boys' Life* magazine, and Scout skits. If you use a Scout skit, you can change characters to fit the size of your den. Your den leader or family members may suggest topics or ideas.

Skits are very short, somewhere between 90 seconds and five minutes long. Brainstorm with your group to decide the best way to present the skit. Keep it simple! Listen to everyone's ideas as you decide on a plan. Each member of your den or family should take part in some way. Who will play each role?

While you plan and practice your skit, keep the Scout Law in mind. Use only language and actions that reflect the beliefs of Scouting and leave everyone—actors and audience—with smiles on their faces.

Practice as a group, and be sure to learn your lines. Remember to speak up so your audience can hear you. How will you make your character come to life with your voice and your gestures?

| Date | Den Leader's OK |

REQUIREMENT 3 | Work together with your den or family to plan, prepare, and rehearse a campfire program to present at a den meeting or pack program.

Now it is time for you to howl! One of the places Scouts howl is at a campfire—a Scouting tradition. A campfire program brings Scouts, parents, and leaders together to have fun!

OPENING

When you gather around a campfire, you will need a way to get everyone's attention so the campfire program can begin. We call this an opening. Openings can be very simple with just reciting the Scout Oath and Scout Law. What are some ways you could open your campfire program?

SONGS

Now that you have completed your opening, it is time to sing a fun song! Think about a song you have sung in your den or pack meetings. Pick one of those or learn a new song.

  A Scout is cheerful. When you laugh and join in at a campfire, you are showing your Scout spirit.

STORY

Near the end of the campfire, someone tells a story. Listening to a story gives everyone a chance to settle down, relax, and enjoy the fading flames of the campfire. The story might be a legend, a tall tale, or a true story. What kinds of stories do you like to hear?

CLOSING

After the story, it is time to close the campfire. With your den leader, choose a way to end your campfire program.

Date	**Den Leader's OK**

REQUIREMENT 4 | Perform your role for a den meeting or pack program.

What role will you play in the program? How will you learn your lines or the words to a campfire song? Sometimes the best way to learn something is just to say it or do it over and over again until you have it. A few minutes of practice can make a big difference in the way you feel when you perform. You might want to practice your lines with someone in your family before you do it for your den or your pack.

There will be many times in Scouting when you will be asked to speak or perform in front of others. The skills you learn will help you in school, in your community, and in your life.

When you work with your den on a campfire program, be trustworthy by doing what you say you will do. Each Wolf needs to "do your best" to make the program great.

_____   _____
Date   **Den Leader's OK**

PAWS ON THE PATH

REQUIRED ADVENTURE

Complete requirements 1–5. Requirements 6 and 7 are optional.

1. Show you are prepared to hike safely in any outdoor setting by putting together the Cub Scout Six Essentials to take along on your hike.

2. Tell what the buddy system is and why we always use it in Cub Scouting. Describe what you should do if you get separated from your group while hiking.

3. Choose the appropriate clothing to wear on your hike based on the expected weather.

4. Before hiking, recite the Outdoor Code and the Leave No Trace Principles for Kids with your leader. (This may be combined with requirement 3 of the Call of the Wild adventure.) After hiking, discuss how you showed respect for wildlife.

5. Go on a 1-mile hike with your den or family. Find two interesting things that you've never seen before and discuss them with your den or family.

6. Name two birds, two insects, and two other animals that live in your area. Explain how you identified them.

7. Draw a map of an area near where you live using common map symbols. Show which direction is north on your map.

SNAPSHOT OF ADVENTURE

Exploring far-away mountains. Traveling through deep, dark jungles. Crossing hot, dry deserts. The adventurers who took these journeys got their start on a short hike, just like the one you and your Wolf den are about to take! In this adventure, you will use your Scouting outdoor skills and learn more about the natural world around you. Hike on, Wolf!

> **REQUIREMENT 1** | **Show you are prepared to hike safely in any outdoor setting by putting together the Cub Scout Six Essentials to take along on your hike.**

The success of a trip often depends on what you carry with you, whether it is in a backpack or on a pack animal.

It is important for you to have items with you to take care of any minor emergencies that could happen, even on a short, 1-mile hike! Cub Scouts who have hiked before you came up with a great list of items to bring. They are called the Cub Scout Six Essentials.

Round up these items, and place them in a backpack before you start out on a hike with your Wolf den.

FIRST-AID KIT

A kit should include a few adhesive bandages, some moleskin (a sticky bandage that you can put over a blister to keep it from getting worse or rubbing), and soap or hand sanitizing gel.

FLASHLIGHT

Check your batteries to make sure they have plenty of power. Your flashlight will be used only in an emergency, so save the batteries for times when you really need them!

FILLED WATER BOTTLE

You should bring enough water for you to drink through your whole hike and back. And make sure your bottle is full when you start out! It is not safe to drink water you find along the trail. Your den leader can help you decide how much water you should bring.

TRAIL FOOD

Trail mix or an energy bar provides quick energy when you need it.

SUN PROTECTION

Sunscreen should be SPF 30 or greater. A hat is good to have, too!

WHISTLE

It's only for emergencies, but a whistle will last longer than your voice.

You might want to pack an extra pair of socks in case your feet get wet or it rains. A rain poncho, waterproof jacket, or even a large plastic garbage bag with holes cut out for your head and arms will keep you dry if it rains. What other gear should you take on your hike? Remember, you'll have to carry it all yourself and bring it all back!

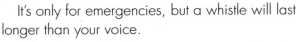

_____   _____
Date   **Den Leader's OK**

REQUIREMENT 2 | Tell what the buddy system is and why we always use it in Cub Scouting. Describe what you should do if you get separated from your group while hiking.

"Two heads are better than one." You may have heard that saying before, and it is true. Sometimes you may forget a safety rule, or not be aware of a hazard up ahead, but if you are with a buddy, it is easier to stay safe.

The buddy system is a great way for Scouts to look after each other, especially on outdoor adventures. When you go hiking, swimming, or camping with your den, each Scout is assigned a buddy. You keep track of what your buddy is doing, and your buddy knows at all times where you are and how you are doing.

A Scout leader might call for a buddy check. That means you must immediately hold up the hand of your buddy. If a Scout is missing, everyone will know it right away. The buddy system is a way of sharing the good times and keeping everyone safe.

My buddy on the hike was: _____

A Scout is brave. When you go hiking, always stay with your buddy and your den. If you do get lost, be brave and stay put until you are found. Learn how to "S-T-O-P" on the next page.

A Wolf should always stay with the rest of the group while hiking. If you do find yourself and your buddy (because you always have one, right?) away from the rest of your den, here is what you need to do:

S - T - O - P!

S = Stay calm. Stay where you are. Sit down, take a drink of water, and eat a little trail food. Stay where you can be seen. Don't hide! You are not in trouble!

T = Think. Think about how you can help your leaders or others find you. Stay where you are, and be sure people can see you. Make yourself an easy target to find. Remember, people will come to look for you. Stay put, be seen, and help them find you!

O = Observe. Listen for the rest of your group or people looking for you. Blow your whistle three times in a row, then listen. Three of any kind of signal means you need help, and everyone will try to help you.

P = Plan. Stay calm, stay put! Plan how to stay warm and dry until help arrives. Don't worry; you will be found.

S – T – O – P! works if you ever get separated from your family, too.

Date   Den Leader's OK

Talk with your den leader about what kind of clothing to wear on the hike. What you need to wear will depend on the season and where you live. It is also important to think about what time of day you will be hiking. Layering is a good way to dress for places where the weather can be cold, hot, and in between, all in one day.

Hat

Layers

Jacket

T-shirt

Shorts

Long pants

Comfortable shoes and socks

Hat

Layers

Jacket

T-shirt

Long pants

Shorts

Comfortable shoes and socks

Date   Den Leader's OK

REQUIREMENT 4 | Before hiking, recite the Outdoor Code and the Leave No Trace Principles for Kids with your leader. (This may be combined with requirement 3 of the Call of the Wild adventure.) After hiking, discuss how you showed respect for wildlife.

Cub Scouts love to be outdoors. But getting to enjoy all of the fun and excitement of nature also means taking care of it.

The Outdoor Code is a way for every Scout to be a part of keeping our world beautiful and safe—today and for years to come.

Read the Outdoor Code below, and practice saying it out loud.

OUTDOOR CODE

As an American, I will do my best to—
Be clean in my outdoor manners,
Be careful with fire,
Be considerate in the outdoors, and
Be conservation-minded.

One of Scouting's principles is "Respect Wildlife."

Read the actions below:

♦ If an action shows respect for wildlife, write **"Yes"** in the box.

♦ If an action does NOT show respect for wildlife, write **"No"** in the box.

Share with your den leader, parent, or other caring adult the choices you made in preparation for your hike in requirement 5.

Action	Respects Wildlife
Chasing a deer off of the path	
Keeping empty snack wrappers to throw away at home	
Watching a bug with a magnifying glass	
Shouting loudly to a friend down the trail	
Leaving wildflowers where you find them	
Feeding some of your snack to a squirrel	

After completing your hike, reflect on the Outdoor Code. With your den leader, discuss ways that you and your den were considerate in the outdoors by respecting wildlife.

Date	Den Leader's OK

REQUIREMENT 5 | Go on a 1-mile hike with your den or family. Find two interesting things that you've never seen before and discuss them with your den or family.

It's time to put your paws on the path and take a hike with your den or your family, Wolf!

Studying a map will help you understand the land and see where you will be hiking. With your family or your den, look at a map of the area where you will be hiking. You might be able to answer these questions.

- Does the trail have a name?
- Is the trail made of dirt, concrete, or another material?
- Is it flat or will you be climbing hills?
- Is there a river, creek, or other body of water around?
- Will you hike in one direction and then turn around and come back, or does the trail make a circle?
- Which direction is north?

Your leader or parent will tell you the rules for hiking. Be sure to follow them so everyone has a great time. You might want to do some leg and arm stretches and a few knee bends before you start out, just to get your body warmed up.

HIKING GUIDELINES

- ◆ Stay on the trail.
- ◆ Walk at a steady pace.
- ◆ Use the buddy system.
- ◆ Give everyone space to enjoy the woods quietly.
- ◆ Stop and rest when needed.
- ◆ Make sure you have your water bottle(s) and drink when you are thirsty.
- ◆ Look and listen for birds, mammals, insects, and other creatures along the way.
- ◆ Use your eyes, ears, and sense of smell to enjoy nature all around you.
- ◆ See if you can spy two interesting things that you have not seen before.

Two interesting things I saw on the trail:

1. _____

2. _____

A Scout is clean. Pack out anything you take with you, and pick up trash you find along the trail.

5

Date   Den Leader's OK

REQUIREMENT 6 | Name two birds, two insects, and two other animals that live in your area. Explain how you identified them.

Wherever you live—in a city, in a suburb, on a farm, by the ocean, or in the mountains—birds, bugs, and other animals live there, too. What kinds of creatures live near you?

With your parent's or guardian's permission, go to the library or on the internet and find information about your local wildlife. Write down two types of birds, two insects, and two other animals that live near you.

BIRDS

Do the birds that you picked live near you all the time or do they migrate (travel) there for part of the year? What do they eat?

What kinds of trees or bushes do they like to nest in? Do both the male and female help build the nest and raise their young?

INSECTS

Are there bees, wasps, ants, flies, roaches, beetles, or butterflies near you? Bugs are fascinating creatures! Did you know that bees can fly up to 60 miles a day to gather food? Or that ants can lift more than 50 times their own weight?

What did you find out about the two insects that you chose?

OTHER ANIMALS

Some wild animals have figured out how to live around people. Coyotes, foxes, possums, raccoons, squirrels, rabbits, deer, and other species of animals may be close by. What kinds of animals live near you?

Tell how the animals you studied can be identified. Share what you found out with your den leader.

Write down the two birds, two insects, and two other animals you learned about that live in your area.

Birds _____

_____

Insects _____

_____

Other animals _____

_____

_____   _____
   Date   **Den Leader's OK**

REQUIREMENT 7 | Draw a map of an area near where you live using common map symbols. Show which direction is north on your map.

A map is a small illustration of a large area of land. Maps can help you figure out where something is located. They can also help you give directions to other people.

Many people look at a map before they start out on a trip so they can visualize (see) where they are going. Some hikers like to look at a computer screen or use a Global Positioning System (GPS) device to help them plan their outing.

With your parent's or guardian's help, look up a map of your town or an area near where you live. Maps use different symbols to show where roads, rivers, lakes, and other large features are located.

The map symbols are shown in a "key," which is a box that tells what they mean. Reading a map is easy when you can use the key. Work with your parent or guardian to learn what the symbols on a map mean.

Look for a compass rose on the map. A compass rose is a circle or a design with points to show directions on a map. Maps are usually oriented toward true north, which will be found at the top of the compass rose.

When north is at the top of the compass rose, south will be at the bottom. East is on the right and west is on the left.

When you draw your map, show which direction is north. You will learn how to use a compass with your den so you can orient a map to north.

Date	Den Leader's OK

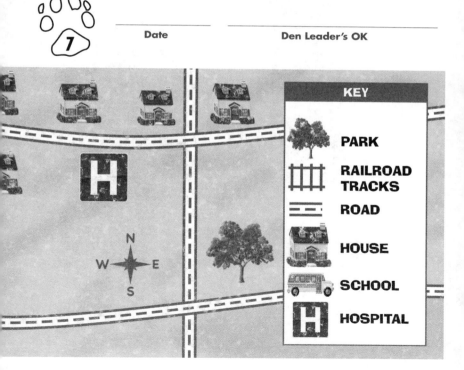

KEY

🌳 PARK

▥ RAILROAD TRACKS

═ ═ ROAD

🏠 HOUSE

🚌 SCHOOL

H HOSPITAL

RUNNING WITH THE PACK

REQUIRED ADVENTURE

Complete the following requirements.

1. Play catch with someone in your den or family who is standing five steps away from you. Play until you can throw and catch successfully at this distance. Take a step back and see if you can improve your throwing and catching skills.

2. Practice balancing as you walk forward, backward, and sideways.

3. Practice flexibility and balance by doing a front roll, a back roll, and a frog stand.

4. Play a sport or game with your den or family, and show good sportsmanship.

5. Do at least two of the following: frog leap, inchworm walk, kangaroo hop, or crab walk.

6. Demonstrate what it means to eat a balanced diet by helping to plan a healthy menu for a meal for your den or family. Make a shopping list of the food used to prepare the meal.

SNAPSHOT OF ADVENTURE

Wolf Scouts lead happy, active lives! Catching, throwing, balancing, and stretching will help you run with your Wolf pack wherever you go. The more you move, the more you will improve! In this adventure, you will practice your Wolf athletic skills and show you know how to eat nutritious food to keep your body running in tip-top shape.

COMPLETE THE FOLLOWING REQUIREMENTS.

> **REQUIREMENT 1** | **Play catch with someone in your den or family who is standing five steps away from you. Play until you can throw and catch successfully at this distance. Take a step back, and see if you can improve your throwing and catching skills.**

When you can follow a ball with your eyes, catch it easily with your hand, and throw it accurately, you are learning a great skill. It is called eye-hand coordination. Before you know it, you will be throwing and catching like a true ball player.

If you have never played catch before, use a soft, squishy ball at first so that nobody gets hurt. If you don't have a baseball glove, you can play catch with your bare hands. Just make sure you use a soft ball, not a baseball, to practice.

HOW TO THROW A BALL

- Gently hold the ball in your throwing hand. Step forward on the opposite foot.
- Bring the ball behind your ear with your elbow pointing backward.

- Turn your body to the side so that the shoulder opposite the ball faces the target. If you are throwing with your right hand, the person catching should be to your left. Never throw a ball with your chest facing the target.
- Point to the other person with your free hand. Then throw. It may take a little practice to throw the ball where you want it to go.

HOW TO CATCH A BALL

- If you are playing with bare hands, reach out with both hands to catch the ball. If you are using a baseball glove, catch the ball in the pocket of the glove. Put your other hand over the ball to keep it from rattling around in the glove or falling out.
- If the ball is thrown to you above your waist, place both of your bare hands in front of your body, fingers up, to catch the ball. Keep your eyes open. If you are using a baseball glove, place the glove in front of your body, glove hand up, to catch the ball. When the ball is inside your glove, put your other hand over the ball to keep it there.
- If the ball comes toward you below your waist, bend at the knees and keep the upper part of your body straight. Watch the ball. Catch the ball with both bare hands in the underhand position or with your glove hand in the underhand position. If you are using a glove, cover the ball with your opposite hand.

PRACTICE PLAYING CATCH!

Once you are comfortable throwing and catching a soft ball, play catch with a family member or someone in your den. If you are playing with bare hands, use a soft, squishy ball for safety. Play catch with a baseball only when you have a baseball glove to catch it.

Start by standing three steps away from someone in your den or family. Throw the ball toward the other person. When the other person catches it, he or she throws it back to you. Each time the ball comes back to you and you catch it, take one step back.

Keep throwing, catching, and stepping back until you are five steps away from the other person. Play until you can catch and throw easily from this distance without dropping the ball on the ground. Then, keep taking steps back after you make a catch. See how far you can go!

Date

Den Leader's OK

REQUIREMENT 2 | Practice balancing as you walk forward, backward, and sideways.

Hiking on a rocky trail. Riding a bike down the street. Walking up and down stairs. These activities all take balance. Balance training is important to everyone, from kids playing games to serious athletes.

Balance helps us stand up straight. It also helps us walk, run, and sit. By practicing balance exercises, you won't fall over as much. And that keeps Cub Scouts in the game!

Here are some exercises to improve your ability to balance:

Walk at least six steps in a straight line on the ground. Go forward and backward. Do it sideways, too. Then try the same steps while walking on a board. Put your arms out to the side to help you stay balanced. Stare at a single focal point, and limit your head and eye movements. This is how tightrope walkers and gymnasts keep their balance.

Another fun activity is to stand up tall, close your eyes, put your hands out to the sides, and hold one leg up for five seconds.

Date	Den Leader's OK

It is fun to do front rolls, back rolls, and frog stands! They also show you are limber and have good balance. Be sure to tuck your chin to your chest when you do front and back rolls. This protects your neck and makes it easier to roll. Do your best!

Frog stand

Front roll

Back roll

_____   _____
Date   Den Leader's OK

REQUIREMENT 4 | Play a sport or game with your den or family, and show good sportsmanship.

Playing sports and games is a great way to be active, and it's also a chance for tons of fun. Choose a sport or game to play with your family or den. Then get your paws moving, Wolf!

While you're playing, remember that Scouts practice good sportsmanship whenever we play together! Good sportsmanship teaches you teamwork, understanding, patience, respect for others, and many more important qualities.

Good sportsmanship means treating those we play with as we would like them to treat us. Use encouraging words, help out your teammates, and be a good winner or loser. This is all part of being a good sport.

Check the ways that you showed good sportsmanship with your family or den.

☐ I stayed calm.

☐ I treated others kindly.

☐ I listened to the adult leaders.

☐ I followed the rules.

☐ I stayed positive.

☐ I encouraged my teammates.

☐ I was friendly after winning or losing.

Remember, good sports have fun because they enjoy playing the game more than they care about the score!

A Scout is friendly. Being a good sport means being friendly and kind to others when you play a sport or a game.

4

_____   _____
Date   **Den Leader's OK**

Walking like different animals lets you use your muscles in different ways. These are fun exercises to try with your den members. They will also help you move quickly, improve your balance, and get stronger. Hop to it, Wolf!

Frog leap

Inchworm walk

Kangaroo hop

Crab walk

Date   Den Leader's OK

Exercise helps keep us strong. So does choosing nutritious food from the five food groups. You don't have to have food from each group at every meal. But you should try to choose foods from each group every day. Talk with your parent or guardian about how you can eat a balanced diet. With his or her help, plan a healthy meal for your family.

There are five food groups: fruits, vegetables, grains, dairy, and protein. You know what fruits and vegetables are. Grains are foods like rice, wheat, oats, cornmeal, and barley, just to name a few. Bread, pasta, and oatmeal are all foods made from grains. The dairy group includes milk, yogurt, and cheese. Meat, chicken, fish, eggs, nuts, and beans are all in the protein group.

The United States Department of Agriculture has made it easier for kids to learn how to choose healthy foods by creating a My Plate chart that shows you what you should eat and how much of your plate should be filled with the five food groups at meals.

Here are some tips to help you plan a good, nutritious meal for your family:

- Eat more fruits and veggies. Make half of your plate fruits and vegetables every day!

- Try whole grains. Ask for oatmeal, whole-wheat breads, or brown rice at meals.

- Rethink your drink. Drink fat-free or low-fat milk or water instead of sugary drinks.

- Focus on lean protein. Choose protein foods like beans, fish, lean meats, and nuts.

- Slow down on sweets. Eat sweets, like cakes or cookies, only once in a while and in small amounts.

Date	Den Leader's OK

ADVENTURES IN COINS

ELECTIVE ADVENTURE

Complete requirements 1–4. Requirements 5–7 are optional.

1. Identify different parts of a coin.

2. Find the mint mark on a coin. Identify the mint where the coin was made and the year it was made.

3. Choose a coin that interests you, and make a coin rubbing. List information next to the coin detailing the pictures on it, the year it was made, and the mint where it was made.

4. Play a game or create a game board with your den or family where you can practice adding and subtracting coins.

5. Play a coin game.

6. Create a balance scale.

7. Do a coin-weight investigation.

SNAPSHOT OF ADVENTURE

To most people, coins are used to buy things they want or need. But coins can also tell a story. The pictures on U.S. coins tell a lot about our country's culture and history.

In this adventure, you will get to be a numismatist (noo-MIZ-muh-tist). Phew! Can you say "numismatist" five times fast? A numismatist is a person who studies coins and money. You'll learn where coins are made and the meaning of their pictures and words. It's time to make some cents, er, sense out of coins!

Look at the stone in the picture. It is a kind of money called a rai stone that weighs thousands of pounds. Can you imagine putting that kind of money in your pocket?

COMPLETE REQUIREMENTS 1–4.
REQUIREMENTS 5–7 ARE OPTIONAL.

REQUIREMENT 1 | Identify different parts of a coin.

Many things have been used for money. Some were useful, like salt, animal hides, and arrowheads, which were traded for other items people needed. Other objects used for money, like shells, had no real value but became symbols of wealth.

Salary is the payment we receive for doing work. The word comes from the Latin word sal, or "salt." In ancient Rome, it meant the amount of money given to a Roman soldier to buy salt.

Even before it was made into coins, metal was used for money. Long ago, each tiny piece of metal had to be weighed every time it was used to figure out its value. Soon, the custom of stamping the weight on the metal became widely used. It made the pieces of metal easier to use for buying and selling things.

While it is a mystery who invented the first coins, experts believe the first coins were minted, or made from metal, in the region around ancient Greece. It wasn't long before many countries were making coins by hand that showed pictures of their rulers and animals.

Modern American coins are made by machines. However, artists design the coins, and scientists work hard to improve how they are made.

Look at a coin. What is special about it? See how many parts you can name.

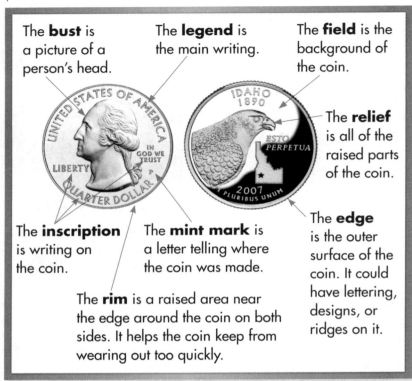

The **bust** is a picture of a person's head.

The **legend** is the main writing.

The **field** is the background of the coin.

The **relief** is all of the raised parts of the coin.

The **inscription** is writing on the coin.

The **mint mark** is a letter telling where the coin was made.

The **edge** is the outer surface of the coin. It could have lettering, designs, or ridges on it.

The **rim** is a raised area near the edge around the coin on both sides. It helps the coin keep from wearing out too quickly.

Ridges on the outer edge of the coin can be felt by rubbing your finger across it. They look like lines imprinted on the side of the coin. The ridges, or milling, were included on coins to keep dishonest people from shaving off the edge of a coin to use the precious metal for other purposes.

Now that you have learned the parts of a coin, share what you learned with your den leader or a parent or guardian.

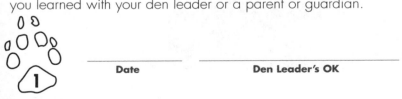

_____   _____
Date   **Den Leader's OK**

Did you know that the U.S. Mint makes 65 million to 80 million coins each day? That's a lot of pocket change!

The job of the U.S. Mint is to make the coins that Americans use. Coins in the U.S. are only made in its secure facilities, while paper money is made in the Bureau of Engraving and Printing.

Most coins have a mint mark, a letter below the date that tells where they were made. Four facilities make coins and use mint marks.

They are:

Philadelphia = P   San Francisco = S

Denver = D   West Point = W

Denver

Today, only the mints in Philadelphia and Denver make circulating coins. (They also make coins for collectors.) Circulating coins are the coins at a bank, in a cash register, or in people's pockets that are used to buy things.

San Francisco

Philadelphia

U.S. Mint
in Denver

The San Francisco and West Point mints only make coins for collectors. These coins could be used as money, but many collectors keep them in their original packaging and never touch them, with the hope that the rare coins will become more valuable over time.

In the past, other U.S. Mint locations made coins. It is possible you might see one of their mint marks on a coin, such as New Orleans, Louisiana, "O"; Charlotte, North Carolina, "C"; and Carson City, Nevada, "CC". You may even find some coins with no mint mark at all!

Now look for the date on the coin. The date of issue is the year the coin was produced. It is usually found on the front of a coin, but on quarters in the 50 State Quarters® Program, the date is on the back of the coin. Isn't it amazing how much you can learn from looking closely at a single coin?

_____   _____
Date   **Den Leader's OK**

REQUIREMENT 3 | Choose a coin that interests you, and make a coin rubbing. List information next to the coin detailing the pictures on it, the year it was made, and the mint where it was made.

You will be amazed at how much detail on a coin comes out when you make a rubbing of it. You can see the incredible amount of work that went into designing, casting, and making a coin.

To make a coin rubbing, you will need:

♦ A pencil or colored pencil

♦ Paper or the chart on page 123

♦ A coin

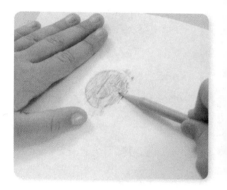

1. Place the paper on top of the coin. Hold the paper firmly, and keep the coin steady.

2. Then, using the side of the pencil lead, rub back and forth across the paper where the coin is lying underneath.

3. Continue rubbing until the entire side of the coin is copied on your paper. Be sure to rub both sides of the coin!

Now find out about the pictures on the coin. Who is this on the front, and what image is on the back? What year was it made, and where was it made?

_____ _____
Date   **Den Leader's OK**

COOL COIN FACTS

Each U.S. coin represents a part of a dollar and shows the faces of famous Americans.

Cent The one-cent coin is often called a penny. The inside of a cent is made with zinc. Then the zinc is coated with copper. The cent features the 16th president, Abraham Lincoln. Some of the designs are shown here.

1909–1958: Two ears of wheat symbolize America's abundance.

1959–2008: One-cent coins have the Lincoln Memorial on the back.

2009: The back shows scenes from Lincoln's life.

 Lincoln's birthplace in Kentucky

 Lincoln as a youth in Indiana

 Lincoln as a lawyer in Illinois

 Lincoln's presidency in the White House

 2010–present: The shield shows the union of states.

Nickel The nickel is worth 5 cents. It is made of copper and nickel, which is how it got its name. It features President Thomas Jefferson and his home, Monticello.

Dime The dime is worth 10 cents and is also made of copper and nickel. It features President Franklin Roosevelt on the front. The back features several items: a torch, which stands for liberty, is in the center; an olive branch for peace is on the left side; and an oak branch for strength is on the right.

Quarter The quarter is worth 25 cents, or one-fourth of a dollar, and is also made of copper and nickel. It features the first U.S. president, George Washington, on the front of the coin. The back of the coin has one of more than 100 different designs, such as a majestic eagle, an outline of a state, U.S. territories, national parks, or the Bicentennial of 1976.

The Bicentennial Quarter celebrates 200 years of American freedom.

State quarters show unique facts about each state.

America the Beautiful Quarters® show national parks and sites in each state; Washington, D.C.; and the U.S. territories.

 U.S. Territories Quarters honor the District of Columbia, Puerto Rico, Guam, American Samoa, U.S. Virgin Islands, and Northern Mariana Islands.

What is on the back of your state's quarter? What does it show about the history or culture of your state?

Half-dollar The half-dollar, or 50-cent piece, is made of zinc and nickel. It features President John F. Kennedy on the front and the eagle from the presidential seal on the back. Before President Kennedy's bust was put on the half-dollar, Benjamin Franklin was featured. The Liberty Bell was on the back of the Franklin half-dollar. This coin was made of 90 percent silver and is rare today.

Dollar The current $1 coin may look like a gold coin, but it is actually made of a special mixture of copper, zinc, manganese, and nickel. There are two coins in circulation today that represent the gold-colored $1 coin.

The Presidential Gallery of gold $1 coins shows a U.S. president on the front and the Statue of Liberty on the back.

Each presidential coin has edge lettering that includes the U.S. motto, "E Pluribus Unum," Latin for "Out of many, one." That means we come from many states but we are united as one country. Turn the coin on its side to see the edge lettering.

Native American gold $1 coins show the contributions of the tribes and individual American Indians to U.S. history and development. Sacagawea is honored on this coin. A Shoshone Indian, she helped Lewis and Clark explore the West all the way to the Pacific Ocean in 1804.

REQUIREMENT 4 | Play a game or create a game board with your den or family where you can practice adding and subtracting coins.

There are many fun counting games you can play with your den or family. Here is one game you can try:

CHANGE MIXER

Materials

- Posters with four different coin names and values written on them, one for each player
- Four orange traffic cones (or chairs) set in a large square
- Music (upbeat)

Instructions

1. Give each player a poster.
2. As the leader plays the music, players walk around the outside of the square.
3. When the music stops, the leader will call out an amount that can be made with the coins.
4. Players must quickly join together at one of the four cones with other players and find the total value of the coins in the group. The goal is for the total value shown on the group's signs to be as close to the value called out as possible.
5. Each group must announce its total correctly. The group that is closest wins the round.

_____   _____
Date   **Den Leader's OK**

You may have played a game of "heads or tails" before, where a person flips a coin up in the air and you call "heads" or "tails." If you call "heads" and the coin lands with the side with the head (or bust) facing up, you win the coin toss.

Coin games have been around just about as long as coins have! Did you know that a coin toss has decided which team will kick off the football game since the start of professional football in 1892?

Now it's time to try a few coin games with your family or den!

Here are two examples you can try:

Coin Basketball Sit down at a table with a large coin, such as a quarter or half-dollar. Place a cup about 2 or 3 feet in front of you. Hold the coin upright on its rim between one finger and thumb. Try tossing the coin into the cup. You can also try bouncing the quarter off a table and into the cup. Just as in basketball, give yourself two points every time you make it in the cup.

Coin Kick Players put a coin on the toe of their shoe. They then raise that foot and "kick" the coin into a pie tin.

_____   _____
          Date   **Den Leader's OK**

REQUIREMENT 6 | Create a balance scale.

Balance scales have been used since ancient times to compare the weight of objects.

You can compare the weights of different coins using a balance scale. It has a horizontal beam from which two pans, plates, or baskets are suspended. When the weights are equal, the beam and pans will hang evenly. When the weight of one item is heavier than the other, the beam will dip to the heavier side.

When coins were made of precious metals, such as silver and gold, the dollar coin was the unit of money. Other coins weighed a fraction, or a part, of a dollar's weight. Even though today's coins are not made of precious metals, the principle still works.

If you use a balance, you will see that four quarters will balance evenly with an Eisenhower dollar coin; two half-dollar coins will balance one Eisenhower dollar coin; and 10 dimes will balance one Eisenhower dollar coin. The 1-cent and 5-cent coins were not made of silver, so they do not follow the rule.

To make a balance scale, you will need:

- ◆ Two paper cups
- ◆ String
- ◆ 10-gallon paint stick
- ◆ Tape
- ◆ Binder clip
- ◆ Pen, pencil, or wooden dowel
- ◆ Heavy book

Instructions

1. Poke holes in two paper cups, and tie strings to them.

2. Hang the paper cups from opposite ends of a 10-gallon paint stick.

3. You will probably want to tape the strings to the stick to keep them from falling off when the beam tilts.

4. Now attach a binder clip to the middle of the stick, dangle it from your fingers, and work the clip back and forth on the stick until the stick hangs level.

5. Hang the binder clip from the pen, pencil, or dowel.

6. Set the pencil on a table, and hold it in place with a heavy book. Your scale is complete!

A Scout is trustworthy. Remember to return any coins you borrow for activities.

_____   _____
Date   **Den Leader's OK**

Using your balance scale, try to find different values of coins that might weigh the same.

For example, do five pennies equal the weight of a nickel? Which is heavier? How can you make them equal? Does the weight of two nickels equal the weight of a dime?

Place a dime on one side of a balance scale and two nickels on the other. Which is heavier? You might also go with your parent or guardian to a bank to ask for a 50-cent coin and an older Eisenhower $1 coin. Then compare them to the other coins. Does the weight of either coin relate to its value?

You can use your balance scale to do many coin-weight investigations.

_____   _____
Date   **Den Leader's OK**

COIN RUBBINGS

You can use this page for the coin rubbings you make for requirement 3.

Coin Rubbing

Type of coin:
Pictures:
Year:
Mint:

Coin Rubbing

Type of coin:
Pictures:
Year:
Mint:

Coin Rubbing

Type of coin:
Pictures:
Year:
Mint:

AIR OF THE WOLF

ELECTIVE ADVENTURE

Complete the following requirements.

1. Conduct two of the following investigations to see how air affects different objects:

   A. Make a paper airplane and fly it five times. Try to make it fly farther by altering its shape. Fly it at least five more times to see if your changes were effective.

   B. Make a balloon-powered sled or a balloon-powered boat. Test your sled or boat with larger and smaller balloons.

Note to Parents and Other Caring Adults

Make sure your Scout does not have an allergy to latex before using balloons for science demonstrations and experiments.

   C. Bounce a basketball that doesn't have enough air in it. Then bounce it when it has the right amount of air in it. Do each one 10 times. Describe how the ball bounces differently when the amount of air changes.

   D. Roll a tire or ball that doesn't have enough air in it, and then roll it again with the right amount of air. Describe differences in how they move.

2. Complete two of the following:

   A. With other members of your den, go outside and record the sounds you hear. Identify which of these sounds is the result of moving air.

   B. Create a musical wind instrument, and play it as part of a den band.

   C. With an adult, conduct an investigation on how speed can affect sound.

D. Make a kite using household materials. With your den or family, explain the rules for safely flying kites. Fly your kite.

E. With your family, den, or pack, participate in a kite derby, space derby, or raingutter regatta. Explain how air helps the vehicle move.

SNAPSHOT OF ADVENTURE

Every day you are surrounded by something that you probably never think about. It's all around you all the time. You need it just like all other living things. It affects the things you do and the games you play. Have you figured out what it is? It's air!

This elective gives you a chance to play with air. This is the air you breathe in and out about 12 to 20 times each minute. It's the air that lets a baseball pitcher throw a curve ball and the air that runs some tools. It's the air that runs wind turbines to create a clean power source. In this adventure, you'll find out how amazing air is! Get ready to try some science investigations, make a paper airplane, and build your own kite.

COMPLETE THE FOLLOWING REQUIREMENTS.

REQUIREMENT 1 | **Conduct two of the following investigations to see how air affects different objects.**

REQUIREMENT 1A | **Make a paper airplane and fly it five times. Try to make it fly farther by altering its shape. Fly it at least five more times to see if your changes were effective.**

HOW TO MAKE A PAPER AIRPLANE

With a single sheet of 8½-by-11-inch paper, you can make an awesome airplane. Look at the diagrams. Follow the steps, and be sure your creases are precise.

See how far your airplane will fly on five separate flights. Now look at your plane. How could you slightly change it to make it go farther? With the help of an adult, look online for free paper airplane patterns that you can print out.

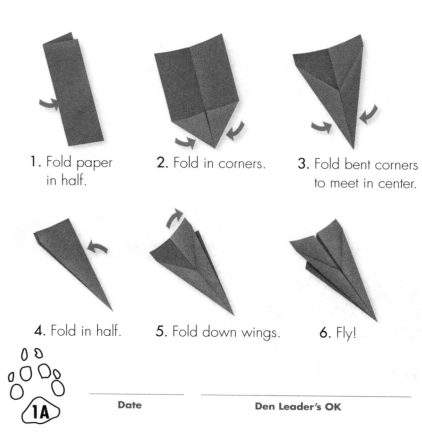

1. Fold paper in half.

2. Fold in corners.

3. Fold bent corners to meet in center.

4. Fold in half.

5. Fold down wings.

6. Fly!

_____   _____
Date   **Den Leader's OK**

HOW TO MAKE A BALLOON-POWERED BOAT

Balloon-powered sleds and boats are fun to make, and they run on air! Here's a balloon-powered boat you can make with help from an adult:

Materials

- Small disposable plastic container
- Sharp knife
- Drinking straw
- Balloon

- Tape
- Small rubber band
- Scissors
- Adhesive putty

Instructions

1. Ask an adult to use the sharp knife to poke a hole in the middle of one end of the container just big enough for your straw to fit through.

2. Cut the straw in half. Attach one end of the straw to the open end of the balloon using tape and wrapping it with the small rubber band. The straw should be attached securely so you can blow up the balloon without air leaking.

3. Thread your straw through the hole in the boat so the balloon end is on the inside of the boat.

4. Use the putty to secure the straw both inside and outside the boat so it is watertight. Now your boat is ready for the water!

5. Using the straw, blow up the balloon and then kink the straw or put your finger on the end of it so the air doesn't escape.

Put the boat in a sink or tub and let go of the straw. Off your boat goes! Try blowing up the balloon a lot and see what happens when you let it go. Try it again, blowing up the balloon a little and seeing your boat go. What was the difference?

1B

_____   _____
Date   **Den Leader's OK**

REQUIREMENT 1C | Bounce a basketball that doesn't have enough air in it. Then bounce it when it has the right amount of air in it. Do each one 10 times. Describe how the ball bounces differently when the amount of air changes.

THAT'S HOW THE BALL BOUNCES!

You will need a hand air pump and a basketball if you choose this requirement. Start with a basketball that isn't completely full of air. Bounce the ball 10 times. Now use the air pump to fill up your basketball with air. Bounce the ball 10 times again.

What did this demonstration teach you about air pressure? The amount of air pressure in a ball has a big effect on how the ball bounces and how high it can bounce. If the ball is properly inflated, the ball will have a higher bounce.

A ball without enough air inside will have a dull bounce. The amount of air pressure determines how much of the ball's surface will hit the ground.

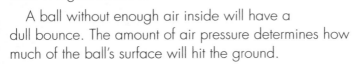

Date	Den Leader's OK

REQUIREMENT 1D | Roll a tire or ball that doesn't have enough air in it, and then roll it again with the right amount of air. Describe differences in how they move.

TO ROLL OR NOT TO ROLL

Air pressure affects the way a tire or a ball handles.

Roll a tire or ball that doesn't have enough air in it. Then roll one that is inflated properly. What did this demonstration show you about air pressure?

Date

Den Leader's OK

REQUIREMENT 2A | With other members of your den, go outside and record the sounds you hear. Identify which of these sounds is the result of moving air.

Did you know that without air there would be no sounds? Sound travels through the air. Moving air pushes things around, and the things it moves create the sounds we associate with wind.

When the wind is blowing at least a little, what sounds can you hear that are caused by the wind? Does it cause the trees to rustle and the grass to swish in the breeze? Does it cause wind chimes to ring? If the wind is blowing fast, does it stop you from hearing other things?

The wind may just be "air," but when air moves, it is a mighty force of nature. It can make sounds when it moves over, around, and through things. It can move things. It can turn wind turbines to make electricity, and farmers can use windmills to pump water for their animals. And if it blows hard enough, such as a tornado or a hurricane, it can even destroy things.

With your den, go outside and record the sounds you hear.

Date   Den Leader's OK

2A

Musical wind instruments can be made from many different types of materials. One way is to use bottles!

Place different amounts of water in several empty bottles. Blow gently across the openings of each bottle. The more water you put in a bottle, the higher the tone will be. The less water you use in a bottle, the lower the sound will be.

With a little practice, you and your den can make music by playing your instruments together. Talk with your den leader about some instruments you can make.

WOODEN HARMONICA

You may want to make a harmonica. Here is what you need to create one.

Materials

- Two tongue depressors or wide craft sticks
- Scissors
- Paper
- Clear tape
- Three rubber bands (one wide, two skinny)

Instructions

1. Cut two strips of paper the same size as a tongue depressor.

2. Place one tongue depressor on top of the other. Wrap one paper strip around each end of the tongue depressors. Wrap tape around each loop without touching the tongue depressors.

3. Slide off one tongue depressor. Stretch the wide rubber band around the length of the tongue depressor and paper loops.

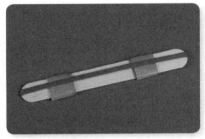

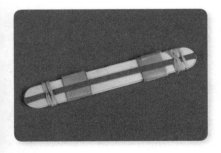

4. Place the second tongue depressor back on top. Wrap one skinny rubber band around each end outside of each paper loop.

5. It's time to make music! Blow air through the middle of your harmonica to play. Slide the paper loops to change the pitch.

Date   **Den Leader's OK**

Working with an adult, swing something hollow around and above your head. Try swinging a cardboard tube tied to a string. Check your safety circle, and be sure no one is close to you!

What happens when you swing the tube faster or slower? If you cut the tube to make it shorter, what happens to the sound?

Date	Den Leader's OK

REQUIREMENT 2D | Make a kite using household materials. With your den or family, explain the rules for safely flying kites. Fly your kite.

Have you ever flown a kite? Did you know that kites have been used for thousands of years and were invented in China? Boys and girls fly kites for fun. Other people use kites, too, including scientists, weather forecasters, and soldiers.

A diamond-shaped kite is easy to fly and will fly even in low wind speeds. Just remember that the larger the paper you use, the better your kite will fly. The heavier the materials you use, the more wind will be needed to get the kite up in the air. Keep your kite lightweight.

HERE ARE SOME BASIC RULES TO FOLLOW TO STAY SAFE WHEN FLYING A KITE:

- Fly kites away from electrical wires.
- Fly kites in fair weather. Put them away if a storm approaches.
- Make kites with paper and wood, never metal—it might attract lightning.
- Use dry string for kite line.
- Fly kites in an open field or park, never on a street or anywhere near a railroad line.
- If a kite gets caught in wires, a tree, or somewhere else, have an adult you know see if it can be retrieved.

HOW TO MAKE A DIAMOND-SHAPED NEWSPAPER KITE

Materials

- Two-page spread of newspaper
- Scissors
- Cellophane tape
- String
- Long sticks, bamboo plant rods, or ¼-inch wooden dowels
- Marker

Instructions

1. Draw the shape of a kite on a double-page spread of newspaper. Cut it out.

2. Lay two sticks across the diamond-shaped newspaper in the shape of a cross. Tape the two sticks together in the center of the cross or use string to tie the two sticks together in the center tightly.

3. Cut the sticks to fit the ends of each corner of the diamond.

4. Make a notch at each of the four corners of the newspaper. Tape all around the outside border of the newspaper to keep the outside edge from tearing in the wind, then tape the wooden cross sticks tightly and securely to the newspaper.

5. Tie a long string onto the middle of the frame and make paper strips for the kite tails. Have fun flying your kite!

A Scout is obedient. Remember to fly your kite in a safe, open area with help from an adult. Be sure to follow the safety rules!

2D

_____   _____
Date   Den Leader's OK

REQUIREMENT 2E | With your family, den, or pack, participate in a kite derby, space derby, or raingutter regatta. Explain how air helps the vehicle move.

There is nothing like a kite derby, space derby, or raingutter regatta to bring out the creative force of Wolf Scouts! There are lots of books and online sites that have great ideas for building cool kites, airplanes, and boats for den and pack competitions. You can also build one of these just for a fun family project. If you decide to make a kite for this requirement, try a design different from the one you created in requirement 2D. Remember to get permission from an adult before going online.

THE SCIENCE OF AIR

Have you ever wondered how air helps a kite stay up? Or how air helps a sailboat slice through the water?

Wind creates lift. Lift is what happens when wind pushes against an object and carries it up. An object's lift depends on the size of its surface. When the wind carries your kite upward, the wind pushes against the whole surface of the kite to lift it up.

Lift also makes sailboats move through the water. Why don't they fly? It's because their sails point up and down, rather than across like a kite or an airplane wing.

2E
Date _____   Den Leader's OK _____

CODE OF THE WOLF

ELECTIVE ADVENTURE

Complete the following requirements.

1. Complete two of the following:

A. With the members of your den or family, make a game with simple materials that requires math to keep score.

B. Play a game of "Go Fish for 10s."

C. Do five activities at home, at school, or in your den that use mathematics, and then explain to your den how you used everyday math.

D. Make a rekenrek with two rows, and show your den leader or other adult how you would represent the numbers 4, 6, 9, and 14.

E. Make a rain gauge or some other measuring device, and use it.

2. Complete one of the following:

A. With other members of your den or family, identify three different types of shapes that you see in nature.

B. With other members of your den or family, identify two shapes you can see in the construction of bridges.

C. Select a single shape or figure. Observe the world around you for at least a week, and write down where you see this shape or figure and how it is used.

3. Complete one of the following:

A. With your den, find something that comes with many small, colored items in one package. Count the number of items of each color in your package. Keep track of each color. Then:

   i. Draw a graph showing the number of items of each color.

ii. Determine what the most common color is.

iii. Compare your results to those of the other Scouts.

iv. Predict how many items of each color you will find in one more package.

v. Decide if your prediction was close.

B. With your den or family, measure the height of everyone in the group and see who takes more steps to walk 100 feet.

C. Have each member of your den shoot a basketball. Count the number of shots it takes for each Scout to sink five baskets. Make a graph that shows how successful your den was. Your graph should show each group that needed 5, 6-10, 11-15, 16-20, and more than 20 tries to sink their shots.

4. Complete one of the following:

A. Use a secret code using numbers to send a message to one of your den members or your den leader. Have that person send a message back to you. Be sure you both use the same code.

B. Send a message to another member of your den or your den leader using the pig pen code or another code that changes letters into special shapes.

C. Practice using a code stick to create and decode a message.

SNAPSHOT OF ADVENTURE

Do you ever think about what you want to do when you grow up? Did you know that everyone uses math, either in a job or in daily activities or both?

In fact, you use math every day—even if you don't think about it. Have you built something recently? You had to count and measure the pieces. Do you have a favorite team? That team keeps score in games. When you buy something, how do you know that you got the correct change?

This adventure helps you to explore how you can use math to have fun.

COMPLETE THE FOLLOWING REQUIREMENTS.

REQUIREMENT 1 | **Complete two of the following:**

REQUIREMENT 1A | **With the members of your den or family, make a game with simple materials that requires math to keep score.**

In many games, you use math to keep score.

Here are some ideas for games you can play with your den or your family members:

- Divide a large piece of cardboard into sections, and mark a number in each section. Try to land paper airplanes on your "aircraft carrier." Add up your points, and the high score wins.

- Mark empty plastic bottles or tin cans with numbers, and roll a ball to see how many you can knock over. Add up your points, and the high score wins.

- Mark a different number in each cell of an egg carton. Mark some with a number to subtract. Drop paper clips or other small objects from above the egg carton. Add up the numbers where the paper clips land. After a few rounds, the high score wins.

- Use clothespins or sticks to make a ring toss game. Clamp clothespins around the rim of a bucket or wastebasket. Toss rubber jar rings at the clothespins from 5 feet away. You can give each clothespin a different number if you would like, or just count the number of ringers. Add up your score after a certain length of time or number of rounds.

| Date | Den Leader's OK |

REQUIREMENT 1B | Play a game of "Go Fish for 10s."

This is just like regular "Go Fish," except the goal is to get two cards that add up to 10. Use a regular deck of cards, but take out all the 10s and face cards. Ace counts as 1.

Start with five cards, and put the extra cards face down on the table. If you have a pair of cards that add up to 10, put them down in front of you.

When it's your turn, ask one player for a card that you can add to one of your cards to make 10. If that player has the card you asked for, put down the pair, and take one card from the deck. If that player doesn't have the card, take one from the deck. Your turn is over when you can make no more pairs that add up to 10. The game ends when you run out of cards.

You might need two decks of cards if there are more than five players.

A Scout is thrifty. If you don't have playing cards, you can make your own deck with index cards.

| Date | Den Leader's OK |

Everyday math is just what it sounds like. You use it every day! For example, you might need to measure something to follow a pattern, or you might need to decide if you have enough money to buy something.

Or you might need to figure out how much silverware you need to set the table for dinner (how many people and how many pieces for each person).

How many plants do you need for a garden if each plant needs a certain space?

What if you want to make a double batch of cookies? How many treats do you need for a den meeting if every Scout gets two treats (plus something for your den leader and assistant den leader)?

Write down five activities where you have used math at home, at school, or in your den, and then share the activities with your den.

Date	Den Leader's OK

The rekenrek was designed in Holland. Its name means arithmetic rack. You can make one with some string, 10 beads of one color, 10 beads of a second color, scissors, and a piece of cardboard.

1. Cut the cardboard to measure 4 inches by 6 inches.

2. With help from an adult, use the tips of scissors to poke two holes at each of the short ends of the cardboard. The holes should be 1½ inches from the edge of the cardboard and 1 inch apart.

3. Cut two pieces of string 8 inches long. Thread the strings through the holes at one side of the cardboard, and tie knots to hold them in place.

4. Add beads to the strings on the other side of the cardboard. Each row of your rack will contain five beads of one color and five beads of another color in the pattern below. That makes 10 beads on each row of your rack.

5. Thread your strings through the other holes. With help from an adult, tie knots to hold the beads in place.

The rekenrek allows you to use different math strategies to come up with the right number or to add and subtract numbers. Start by placing all the beads on the right side of the rack.

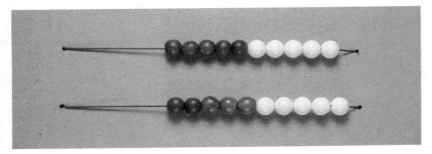

As you count the number of beads you need to show a number, push the beads you counted over to the left. Let's say the number you are asked to find is 5. You know that you have five beads of one color and five beads of another color on each line of your rack. You would simply push the first five beads of one color on the first row over to the left. You have just shown the number 5 on the rekenrek. Or you could count by ones to make five beads on the left.

Now show Akela how you would represent the numbers 4, 6, 9, and 14.

With help from an adult, you can make a rain gauge. You will need a plastic soda bottle, colored tape, a ruler, scissors, and a pencil or marker.

1. Cut off the top of the bottle where the curved top meets the straight sides.

2. Turn the top upside down and fit it into the base. This will stop the water inside the bottle from evaporating. Drop in several small stones, and fill the base with 1 inch of water. You will measure from this starting point.

3. Add a thin strip of tape around the base at the starting point. Then add a vertical tape strip for measuring rain. Mark 1/8-inch divisions on the measuring tape strip.

4. Place your rain gauge outside, away from any buildings and trees. Record the amount of rain each day for at least a week, and remember to refill or pour out the water down to the starting point each morning.

_____   _____
Date   **Den Leader's OK**

REQUIREMENT 2 | Complete one of the following:

REQUIREMENT 2A | With other members of your den or family, identify three different types of shapes that you see in nature.

Do you ever notice different shapes around you? Sometimes a shape can help you identify something (for example, the shape of a bird's tail).

With members of your den, make a list of all the shapes you can think of. Then take a short hike to see how many different shapes you can find in leaves, flowers, trees, rocks, clouds, and grass.

Sometimes, the shapes are made of repeating patterns, such as in the leaves of ferns.

What shape are dandelion flowers? Can you find a leaf that is heart-shaped or an oval? What shape are the nests that birds make? Have you ever looked carefully at a bee's honeycomb? Share the shapes you find in nature with your den leader or a parent or guardian.

Date	Den Leader's OK

Bridges make it possible to cross over water or other natural barriers, such as canyons. The first bridges were simple stepping-stones placed over a small stream to help people get to the other side. Using the stones as a base, people were able to build a better bridge by placing a toppled tree, a log, or a wooden plank over the stones.

Three common types of bridges are arched bridges, beam bridges, and suspension bridges.

The most common shapes used to build bridges are squares, triangles, and cylinders. The triangle is the strongest shape. Triangles are used to make a very strong form called a truss.

Another strong shape is a cylinder. If you look at your bicycle, you can see that cylinders are used to make the frame strong. They are also used to make piers underneath bridges strong enough to hold a lot of weight. Squares are weaker and can collapse unless the angles are braced. Squares in bridges are braced with triangles to make them stronger.

Take some photos, find some photos, or draw pictures of different bridges. What shapes do you see in the bridges? Are all bridges built the same? Are the shapes different depending on how big the bridge is? Be sure you look at all the shapes, even the smallest parts of the bridge. Identify two shapes used in the bridges you saw. Show your den what you have found, and tell them why you think a certain shape was used.

2B

_____   _____
Date   **Den Leader's OK**

When artists look at scenes they would like to paint, they may look at them differently than you and I would. They see the pictures in different shapes they can draw. Now you can look at the world around you the way an artist does! What shapes do you see?

Squares and rectangles are easy, and you'll see them all around your house. But you might also see squares in squares (windows) or circles in circles (basketballs through a hoop). Do you see more square, rectangular, or circular clocks? What shape is a bird's beak or the point of your pencil?

Pick a single shape that you like, and write down each time you see it for a week. Share with your den leader or a parent or guardian where you found this shape and how it was used.

_____   _____
Date   Den Leader's OK

REQUIREMENT 3A | With your den, find something that comes with many small, colored items in one package. Count the number of items of each color in your package. Keep track of each color. Then:

i. **Draw a graph showing the number of items of each color.**

ii. **Determine what the most common color is.**

iii. **Compare your results to those of the other Scouts.**

iv. **Predict how many items of each color you will find in one more package.**

v. **Decide if your prediction was close.**

Do you ever wonder how predictions are made about the weather? The people who make the predictions have noticed that when one thing happens, another thing is more likely to happen. So if it rained 100 miles away yesterday, it might be more likely to rain where you are today.

Of course, those are just predictions, and they could be wrong. That's why the weather forecasters say there's a chance of rain or snow or sun; they don't guarantee that it will rain or snow or be sunny.

You can make predictions about what is likely and what is unlikely based on your own observations. With your den, select an item to count. You can use colored paper clips, marbles, a small bag of different colored candies, or a snack or cereal with different colored pieces. Count the number of objects of each color in your own package of the item. Then create a graph to show your results and compare your graph to those of the other Wolf Scouts.

Use the results to make a prediction about how many items of each color you will find in one more package. This is called probability. You can never know exactly what will happen, but you will have a better idea of what to expect based on the results of your investigation.

How close was your prediction? How close did the other Scouts in your den get to an accurate prediction? Share what you have learned with your den leader or a parent or guardian.

3A

Date   **Den Leader's OK**

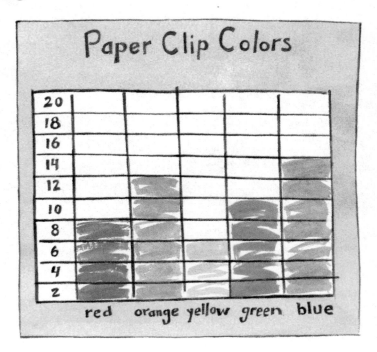

With your den or your family, mark a starting line and a finish line at least 100 feet apart. Have each person walk from the starting line to the finish line, and count the number of steps he or she takes. Next, measure how tall each person is.

What do you notice? Does everyone take the same number of steps? Who took the most steps? Who took the fewest steps? Do you think it takes more steps or fewer steps if you are taller or shorter?

_____   _____
Date   **Den Leader's OK**

Using a graph like the one shown in this picture, show how many shots it takes each person in your den to make five baskets.

With an adult's help, find out what your shooting percentage is by dividing the number of baskets by the number of shots you took.

Remember, a Scout is cheerful. Keep a positive attitude (even if basketball is hard for you), and encourage your Wolf friends. Have fun, and do your best!

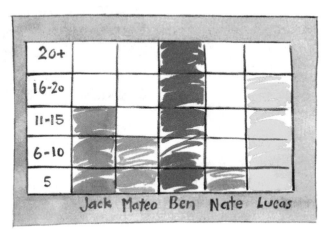

Date

Den Leader's OK

REQUIREMENT 4A | Use a secret code using numbers to send a message to one of your den members or your den leader. Have that person send a message back to you. Be sure you both use the same code.

What would you do if you had to send a secret message to someone else—a message that no one else should know? You could make up a secret code using math and use a different number for each letter. Then, if someone doesn't know the code, they can't read your message.

People who have to send secret messages do just that. That's another reason to know math—so you can send secret messages or crack someone else's code.

You can find lots of cool codes online (with a parent's permission) and in books. Look for beginner codes that use numbers and then teach the code to one of your den members or your den leader. Send a message in code to the person and see if you can read the message they send back to you!

<u>4A</u>   _____   _____
                   Date   **Den Leader's OK**

Besides numbers, shapes can also be used to stand for letters. In the pig pen code, the alphabet is copied into grids. Then, each part of the "pig pen" is substituted for the letter in that part. For the second grid of each type, dots are added.

So, the letter "A" is and the letter "W" is .

The pig pen code shapes are below:

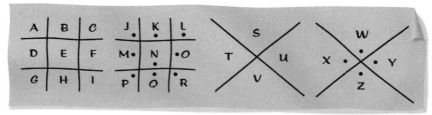

Practice with this message:

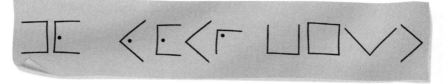

Send a message to another member of your den or your den leader using the pig pen code or another code that changes letters into special shapes.

Date   **Den Leader's OK**

A code stick is another fun way to create secret messages. It was used by the Romans in ancient times to send secret messages during times of war. An enemy warrior who stole the secret message would not be able to read it.

CODE STICK

Materials
- Piece of paper
- Scissors
- Pencil to wrap the paper around
- Pencil or pen to write with
- Tape

Instructions
1. Cut a long, thin strip of paper about ¼ to ½ inch wide from the side of a sheet of paper.

2. Tape the piece of paper to the top of a pencil. Wrap it tightly around the length of the pencil so the edges of the strip are exactly side by side.

3. Tape the paper strip to the other end of the pencil so the paper strip stays in place when you write on it.

4. Write your secret message down one side of the pencil. Add a few extra letters on other sides.

5. Unwrap the strip of paper from the pencil. The letters should be mixed up and seem random. Pass the secret code to another Wolf.

6. Your Wolf buddy should be ready to wrap the paper strip around a pencil to decode it. The letters will now form the secret message.

See if you can send a message made on a code stick and decode a message sent back to you by a friend!

Date   **Den Leader's OK**

COLLECTIONS AND HOBBIES

ELECTIVE ADVENTURE

Complete the following requirements.

1. Begin a collection of 10 items that all have something in common. Label the items and title your collection.

2. Share your collection at a den meeting.

3. Complete one of the following and tell your den what you learned:

   A. Visit a show or museum that displays different collections or models.

   B. Watch a webcast or other media presentation about collecting or model building.

4. Complete one of the following:

   A. Create an autograph book, and get 10 autographs. Start with members of your den.

   B. With your parent's or guardian's permission, pick a famous living person, and write him or her a letter. In your letter, ask the person to send you an autographed photo.

SNAPSHOT OF ADVENTURE

A hobby is something you enjoy doing in your spare time. Building model airplanes. Model railroading. Reading. Singing. Playing a musical instrument. Leather crafting. Stargazing. Fishing. The list of hobbies is endless.

You can collect just about anything, too. Miniature toy cars. Lunch boxes. Patches. Baseball cards. Stamps. Coins. Postcards. Drawings. You may already have a group of one of your favorite things at home, but you've never called it a collection.

Now it's time to explore what you are interested in, fascinated by, amazed at, and like a lot. Start collecting, Wolf!

COMPLETE THE FOLLOWING REQUIREMENTS.

REQUIREMENT 1 | Begin a collection of 10 items that all have something in common. Label the items and title your collection.

Collecting things is a neat way to celebrate who you are. You may choose to collect something that has special meaning to you or makes you happy. What you collect is done for your own enjoyment, so it can be whatever you like!

Keep in mind that collections don't have to cost a lot. Some people collect soda bottle caps, colored bottles, autographs, movie and concert posters, and many other items that are free. Others collect fishing lures, key chains, ceramic dogs, action figures, marbles, and other items that don't cost a lot of money.

People who collect things over time often gain new skills and learn about the objects they enjoy. Collectors enjoy spending free time finding, organizing, and sharing their collections.

Some collectors are generalists. That means they collect a wide range of things— for example, stamps from all over the world. Other collectors are very specific in what they collect, such as only postage stamps from the 1800s.

It may sound funny, but some people collect experiences instead of objects! For example, birders collect the names of the species of birds they have spotted. People who love to travel collect stamps in their passports from visiting foreign countries. Others visit all the state parks or the national parks or all the roller coasters or putt-putt courses they can, and collect bumper stickers or photos. They basically collect memories!

Gather 10 items that follow the same theme. Then, label them and think of a title for your collection. Think about why you enjoy collecting this item and what items you might like to add over time. If you collect trips or experiences with your family, you could label and title the photographs, postcards, or other souvenirs.

Date

Den Leader's OK

REQUIREMENT 2 | Share your collection at a den meeting.

Before you bring your collection to share, jot down a few notes to answer the questions below. This will help you remember what you want to tell the den about the items you collect. Tell your den the following things about your collection:

- ◆ What did you collect?
- ◆ Why did you choose that collection?
- ◆ Where did you find the items for your collection?
- ◆ How will you add to your collection?

It's fun to share a collection with your den. When you share your interests with your Wolf friends, it gives them a chance to learn more about the person you are and what you like to do. If it's too difficult to bring your actual collection to a den meeting, you can present it another way, such as with photographs.

A collection of Scout patches is great to share at a den meeting.

A Scout is courteous. Remember to listen carefully and be supportive as the other Wolves share their interests and collections, too.

It would be a pretty boring world if everyone's interests were exactly the same. Have fun celebrating everyone's different interests! Every individual in your den brings something special to your group. What did you learn about the other members of your den when they shared their collections?

_____   _____
Date   **Den Leader's OK**

REQUIREMENT 3A | Visit a show or museum that displays different collections or models.

Museums are places where many valuable and interesting collections are displayed for the public. There are antique car museums, train museums, toy museums, art museums, military museums, historical museums, science and space museums, and museums that display the belongings or the historic homes of important people. Some museums tell the story of a town's history. Or they may tell of an important industry, such as mining or ranching.

When you visit a museum near you with your family or den, find out what the museum specializes in collecting. See if you can pick up a brochure that tells more about the museum. If you have questions about the items on display, ask a museum volunteer or staff member. They will be happy to help you understand what the museum is all about.

Share what you learned about the museum and its collection with your den.

Date	Den Leader's OK

REQUIREMENT 3B | Watch a webcast or other media presentation about collecting or model building.

An interesting and fun way to learn more about a hobby or type of collection you might be interested in is, with your parent's or guardian's permission, to watch a video presentation explaining the activity. Introductory programs on all sorts of hobbies and collections can be found on the internet, at your local library, or even at the museum you may have visited in requirement 3A. Share with your den what you learned about your chosen hobby or collection while watching the media presentation.

Date	Den Leader's OK

REQUIREMENT 4A | Create an autograph book, and get 10 autographs. Start with members of your den.

The hobby of collecting autographs is known as philography (fi-LOG-ruh-fee). Some people collect autographs because they like the people and any work they may have done. Others collect autographs in the hope that one day the autographs might be worth money. Autographs can be found on almost anything from plain paper to baseballs to musical instruments.

Collecting an autograph

You can create your own simple autograph book using white paper. Make a cover out of construction paper or card stock, decorate it with markers or colored pencils, and turn it into a book by adding a split ring or by stapling the pages together.

Ask for the autographs of your den members, your friends and family, or your coaches and teachers. Show your den leader your autograph book.

Date   **Den Leader's OK**

When you write a letter to a famous person, it doesn't have to be long but it should have a beginning, middle, and end.

Here is how you should set up your letter:

Today's Date

Mr./Mrs./Ms./Miss/Dr. and the person's full name
Street Address
City, State, Zip Code

Greeting,

First, tell the person why you are writing a letter. Be polite.

Then, tell why you enjoy what the person does or how you support what they do. Tell a little about yourself, too, and that you are working on your Wolf rank in Cub Scouts.

Finally, say that you would appreciate it if they could send you an autographed photo. Explain that you have enclosed a self-addressed, stamped envelope for them to send you the photo. End by thanking them for their time.

Then sign your letter:

Sincerely,

Your Name
Your Street Address or P.O. Box
City, State, Zip Code

Your parent, guardian, or den leader may be able to help you find an address for the person you choose to write. Remember to enclose a large, self-addressed, stamped envelope when you send your request.

It may take a couple of months before you receive a reply from a famous person. Good luck!

| Date | Den Leader's OK |

CUBS WHO CARE

ELECTIVE ADVENTURE

Complete at least four of the following requirements.

1. With other members of your den, try using a wheelchair or crutches, and reflect on the process.

2. Learn about a sport that has been adapted so that people in wheelchairs or with some other physical disability can play, and tell your den about it.

3. Learn about "invisible" disabilities. Take part in an activity that develops an understanding of invisible disabilities.

4. With your den, try doing three of the following things while wearing gloves or mittens:

   A. Tying your shoes

   B. Using a fork to pick up food

   C. Playing a card game

   D. Playing a video game

   E. Playing checkers or another board game

   F. Blowing bubbles

5. Draw or paint a picture two different ways: Draw or paint it once the way you usually would and then again while using a blindfold. Discuss with your den the ways the process was different.

6. Use American Sign Language to communicate either a simple sentence or at least four points of the Scout Law.

7. Learn about someone famous who has or had a disability, and share the person's story with your den or family.

8. Attend an event where people with disabilities are participants or where accommodations for people with disabilities are made a part of the event.

SNAPSHOT OF ADVENTURE

This adventure will help you and your fellow Wolf Scouts understand just how many things people with disabilities are able to do. You will discover some challenges people with disabilities face, and you will have the chance to try facing similar challenges yourself. You can also learn about one amazing person who didn't let a disability stand in the way of a dream.

COMPLETE AT LEAST FOUR OF THE FOLLOWING REQUIREMENTS.

REQUIREMENT 1 | With other members of your den, try using a wheelchair or crutches, and reflect on the process.

A single activity can't show you everything about life with a disability, but it can help you understand a little more about the ways a person with a disability is able to do things.

For this requirement, try using a wheelchair or crutches to get around and think about the skills people with physical disabilities develop to be able to use wheelchairs or crutches.

Is using a wheelchair or crutches easy or hard? Does it make your hands or arms tired? What would you do if you had to go up the stairs? What if you had to go up or down a hill in a wheelchair? How would you get in and out of a car without help if you couldn't use your legs? Also consider the challenges you encountered and what could be done to overcome them. Talk with your den leader about what you learned.

_____   _____
Date   Den Leader's OK

"I don't need easy. I just need possible," said Bethany Hamilton, a surfer who reached her dream of surfing professionally even after losing one arm.

Athletes with disabilities have the same desires that able-bodied athletes do. They want to do their best and compete with others. They want to show their independence and will to succeed. Jim Abbott is a former major league baseball pitcher who was born without a right hand. He said that people should focus on what an athlete can do instead of on a disability.

Organized sports for people with physical disabilities started after World War II, when people injured in the war played sports to help them heal. Today, there are many adaptive sports, which are also called parasports. The Paralympics is a competition for disabled athletes from around the world. A few athletes with disabilities have also competed in events in the Olympic Games, and some are active in professional sports.

Disabled Sports USA helps wounded warriors, children, and adults become active. It has become one of the largest organizations for disabled athletes in America.

Did you know that basketball, football, hockey, rugby, soccer, and many other sports have been adapted so people in wheelchairs can play? Archery, handcycling, powerlifting, shooting, swimming, table tennis, and track and field events are just some of the many other sports that people with physical disabilities compete in.

In recent years, many disabled athletes have also started competing in extreme sports, such as kayaking, skateboarding, surfing, and rock climbing.

Learn about one sport that has been adapted for people with disabilities. Do you have other ideas for ways that you could change a sport? Share with your den what you learned.

Date   Den Leader's OK

REQUIREMENT 3 | Learn about "invisible" disabilities. Take part in an activity that develops an understanding of invisible disabilities.

Some people have disabilities that others can see, such as disabilities that require a wheelchair, while other disabilities are "invisible," which means that others might not see them.

Invisible disabilities, such as autism or attention deficit/ hyperactivity disorder (ADHD), can include those that cause people to think or feel things differently than those without the disability. Many children with invisible disabilities

are successful in school and activities with some adaptations, or changes, to better fit how they learn.

It can be hard for people to understand what it is like to have an invisible disability. With your den, take part in an activity to help you better understand some types of these disabilities. Some activities will help you understand the spectrum, or range, of autism disorders and how each person with autism is different. After the activity, talk with your den leader about what you learned.

Date   Den Leader's OK

REQUIREMENT 4 | With your den, try doing three of the following things while wearing gloves or mittens:

REQUIREMENT 4A | Tying your shoes

REQUIREMENT 4B | Using a fork to pick up food

REQUIREMENT 4C | Playing a card game

REQUIREMENT 4D | Playing a video game

REQUIREMENT 4E | Playing checkers or another board game

REQUIREMENT 4F | Blowing bubbles

How important are your hands to you? When you try to do everyday things with gloves or mittens on, you may get a better idea of how much you depend on your hands.

Do the gloves or mittens make it harder to do basic things? Is it just because the gloves or mittens get in the way, or is it because you can't feel what you are trying to do? Would you have to learn how to do things differently if you couldn't use your hands? How would you feel if someone made fun of you because you couldn't do certain things?

People with disabilities find ways to overcome challenges every day. They also must deal with people who do not understand the difficulties they have and say things that are thoughtless.

A Scout is kind. Remember to treat all people as you would like to be treated. If you see someone with a disability who is having trouble picking up an item or opening a door, ask if you can help!

Date	**Den Leader's OK**

REQUIREMENT 5 | Draw or paint a picture two different ways: Draw or paint it once the way you usually would and then again while using a blindfold. Discuss with your den the ways the process was different.

You probably count on your eyes to tell you a lot about the world. People who are blind or visually impaired use other senses to give them information about the world around them. They develop an understanding of colors through ideas such as "blue is a cool color, like a glass of water" or "the sun is warm, and yellow and orange are warm colors." They can focus on shape, texture, and size to create an image.

For this requirement, draw or paint a picture. Then put on a blindfold and draw or paint the same picture. Get help from one of the members of your den, who may need to guide you to the correct color or to the paper. If you are a helper, think carefully about words and actions that will guide your friend.

When you are finished, think about how it felt different to draw or paint without sight. Did you focus more on the movement of the crayon or marker or how you felt as you painted? Did you think differently about the colors you chose? Did your helper guide you clearly? How could you be a better helper if someone you know is visually impaired or blind? Discuss your experience with your den.

_____   _____
Date   Den Leader's OK

How do you use your sense of hearing every day? It is probably an important part of the way you communicate with others. If you couldn't hear someone talking to you, how would you know what the person was saying? Do you think it would be hard to talk if you couldn't hear the sounds you were making? How would you pronounce a word if you had never heard it before?

Many people who are deaf or hard of hearing use American Sign Language (ASL) to communicate. ASL is a visual language (a language you can see) that uses gestures, along with facial expressions and body language, instead of spoken words. It takes practice to learn ASL, but you can start with just a few signs.

Loyal   Friendly   Cheerful   Clean

Learn a simple sentence or four points of the Scout Law in American Sign Language. Teach one of the members of your den the words you learned. Maybe these signs will be just the beginning of learning a new language!

_____ _____
Date **Den Leader's OK**

186 ▪ Wolf

Many people who aren't famous live with and work to overcome their disabilities every day of their lives. Others have made incredible contributions to society as actors, athletes, and world leaders, and in many other professions and fields.

Here are some people you might want to learn about:

Thomas Edison, inventor of the light bulb, the motion picture, audio recording, and more, experienced a hearing loss.

Jean Driscoll won the Boston Marathon wheelchair division eight times and won 12 medals in the Paralympic Games. She was born with spina bifida.

Franklin Roosevelt, the 32nd president of the United States, was paralyzed from the waist down by polio. He was active as a Scout leader and received the Silver Buffalo Award.

 Stephen Hawking, a famous scientist and author, was diagnosed with Lou Gehrig's disease (ALS) when he was only 21 years old.

Helen Keller, famous author and lecturer, was deaf and blind.

Share the story of the person you learned about with your den. How did the person's story inspire you?

Date

Den Leader's OK

With your den or your family, attend an event where people with disabilities are participants. You may find a local sporting event, such as one where deaf athletes compete, or one sponsored by Easter Seals or Special Olympics. You may also choose to attend a performance or presentation in which an interpreter uses sign language. You may find an art show or an event that includes the work of people with and without disabilities.

Share what you learned about your experience with the members of your den.

AXIS Dance Company performance

Date   Den Leader's OK

8

DIGGING IN THE PAST

ELECTIVE ADVENTURE

Complete the following requirements.

1. Play a game that demonstrates your knowledge of dinosaurs, such as a dinosaur match game.

2. Create an imaginary dinosaur. Share with your den its name, what it eats, and where it lives.

3. Complete one of the following:

   A. Make a fossil cast.

   B. Make a dinosaur dig. Be a paleontologist, and dig through a dinosaur dig made by another member of your den. Show and explain the ways a paleontologist works carefully during a dig.

4. Make edible fossil layers. Explain how this snack is a good model for the formation of fossils.

SNAPSHOT OF ADVENTURE

Can you imagine birds the size of airplanes flying over your head? How about animals like one of the largest dinosaurs, *Argentinosaurus*—100 tons and 120 feet long—walking through your neighborhood? Can you picture what it would be like to run into a big, bad *T. rex* in the woods? Yikes! Dinosaurs and other giant creatures lived and died out millions of years ago, so thankfully they won't be running by your home anytime soon!

Paleontologists study dinosaur bones and fossils to learn more about their habits, the food they ate, and their size. During this adventure, you will match dinosaurs to their names, and you'll use your imagination to create your own dinosaur.

> **REQUIREMENT 1 | Play a game that demonstrates your knowledge of dinosaurs, such as a dinosaur match game.**

Millions of years ago, there were many types of dinosaurs and ancient reptiles. There were dinosaur herbivores (plant eaters) and carnivores (meat eaters), plus plesiosaurs (PLEE-see-uh-sawrs) (sea creatures) and pterosaurs (TER-uh-sawrs) (flyers).

Read about some of these creatures below. Then try to match the correct creature to the clues.

You may also play a dinosaur match game with your den or your family members. Give out cards with dinosaur facts on them to half of the people playing the game. Give out cards with pictures of the dinosaurs to the other half. Have players find their match. You can also have an adult cover up the pictures and names for each creature in your handbook. Then, see if you can use the fast facts to guess the names.

HERBIVORES (PLANT EATERS)

Apatosaurus
(uh-PA-tuh-sahr-us)

Fast Facts:
♦ Mistakenly called *Brontosaurus*
♦ Name means "deceptive lizard"
♦ One of the largest land animals, 70 to 90 feet long, 15 feet tall, weighed 30 to 35 tons
♦ Fossils found in Wyoming, Colorado, Oklahoma, and Utah
♦ Featured a long neck, four legs, and a long, whip-like tail

Triceratops
(tri-**SAIR**-uh-tops)

Fast Facts:
- Name means "three-horn face"
- Lived in western North America
- Featured a large bony frill and three horns on its face
- Was a snack for *T. rex*
- Weighed 4 to 6 tons

Ankylosaurus
(**ANG**-ki-lo-sawr-us)

Fast Facts:
- Name means "fused lizard"
- Lived in North America
- Featured a triangular-shaped head, a heavily armored body, and back legs longer than its front legs
- Used its long heavy club tail to break the legs of enemies

Parasaurolophus
(par-uh-**SAWR**-ol-uh-fus)

Fast Facts:
- Name means "near crested lizard"
- Featured a large crest on its head almost 6 feet long
- Fossils found in Canada, New Mexico, and Utah

CARNIVORES (MEAT EATERS)

Tyrannosaurus rex
(tuh-RAN-uh-SAWR-us)

Fast Facts:

- Name means "tyrant lizard"
- Lived in forested river valleys in North America
- Featured huge teeth, strong back legs, short front legs, and powerful tail
- Was 40 feet long and 15 to 20 feet high
- Ate other dinosaurs—scientists believe it could eat 500 pounds in a single bite

Spinosaurus
(SPY-nuh-sawr-us)

Fast Facts:

- Name means "spine lizard"
- Featured fan-shaped spine on its back, short front legs, and powerful back legs
- The largest carnivore and may have been longer than *T. rex*
- Lived on land and in water
- Ate fish and other small and medium-sized prey

Velociraptor
(veh-loss-ih-RAP-tor)

Fast Facts:

◆ Name means "speedy thief"

◆ Hunted in packs

◆ Could run up to 40 miles per hour in short bursts

◆ Featured a sharp, curved claw on each foot

◆ Weighed about 33 pounds

◆ Ate small animals such as reptiles, amphibians, and smaller, slower dinosaurs

BIRDS

Hesperornithiformes
(hes-pur-or-NITH-uh-formz)

Fast Facts:

◆ A group of birds with feathers that weren't used for flying but kept them warm

◆ Lived mostly in water

◆ Had teeth and ate fish

◆ Featured webbed feet far back on their bodies for diving

◆ Fossils found in western North America, Europe, Mongolia, and Kazakhstan

◆ May have come on land only to nest and lay eggs

Archaeopteryx
(ar-kee-OP-tuh-riks)

Fast Facts:

◆ Name means "ancient wing"

◆ Considered to be the oldest known bird

◆ Lived in southern Germany

◆ Featured sharp teeth and three fingers with claws on each wing

◆ Similar in size to a raven

◆ Ate lizards, frogs, and beetles

PTEROSAURS (FLYERS)

Pteranodon
(tuh-RAN-uh-dawn)

Fast Facts:

◆ Name means "winged tooth"

◆ Flying reptile (not a dinosaur)

◆ Wings spanned 18 feet

◆ Featured hollow bones

◆ Fossils found in Kansas and England

◆ Ate fish and the carcasses of dinosaurs and other animals

Study the traits of each dinosaur or dinosaur relative, and see if you can match the correct creature to the facts in the "Who am I?" box.

A Scout is friendly. Playing games is a great way to make a new friend or have fun with an old one!

Who am I?

1. My protection comes in the form of spines on my body and a long heavy club tail that could be used to break the legs of enemies.

_____ *Apatosaurus*

_____ *Triceratops*

2. I am longer than the *T. rex*; I have a sail on my back, and scientists think I speared fish out of the water.

_____ *Ankylosaurus*

3. I weigh about 4 tons and have a bony crest on my head.

_____ *Parasaurolophus*

4. I am only about 12 inches long and have three fingers with claws on each of my wings.

_____ *Tyrannosaurus*

5. I am small and fast. I have sharp claws on my front and hind feet.

_____ *Velociraptor*

6. I have three horns and a bony frill with points on its edges.

7. I use my webbed feet to dive for fish.

_____ *Spinosaurus*

8. I am a carnivore with little arms and a big bite.

_____ *Archaeopteryx*

9. I am a reptile that lived alongside dinosaurs. I was able to fly because I was very light—my hollow bones were filled with air sacs.

_____ *Pteranodon*

10. I am one of the largest land animals. I have a long neck and eat only plants.

_____ *Hesperornithiformes*

Share with your den other information you might know
about dinosaurs.

_____   _____
Date   Den Leader's OK

Now you can make up your own dinosaur using your imagination! A Scout is thrifty, so create one out of recycled objects and common craft items.

Some items you can use include water bottles, laundry soap bottles, soda cans, bottle caps, cereal boxes, container lids, chenille stems, buttons, clay, papier-mâché, cardboard tubes, spools, construction paper, and felt! Remember to ask an adult before you use any of the materials you collect.

Share your dinosaur with your den. Remember, your dinosaur is your own unique creation. Don't forget to make up a name for your dinosaur and tell where it lived and what it ate.

Date	**Den Leader's OK**

REQUIREMENT 3A | Make a fossil cast.

Fossils are the remains or impression of a prehistoric organism, or living thing, preserved in earth or rock. Examples of fossils include skeletons, leaf prints, or footprints embedded in the earth's crust.

> Fossils and historical artifacts can be found anywhere. Two of the few known *Tyrannosaurus rex* tracks in the world were discovered at Philmont Scout Ranch, the first in 1983 and the second in 2009. Philmont is located in the Rocky Mountains, near Cimarron, New Mexico.
>
> You might have a chance to see the tracks in person if you take a backpacking trip to Philmont when you become an older Scout.

Some fossils, like the *T. rex* footprints at Philmont Scout Ranch, formed when a dinosaur stepped onto soft ground and left a print. When the ground hardened, a fossil formed. Today, you will have the chance to make your own fossil!

Instead of soft ground, you will use air-dry clay. Roll your clay into a ball in your hand. Pat it down on a paper plate to flatten it out to at least ½ inch thick. It is OK if it looks a little bit lumpy. The ground is lumpy too.

Press a leaf, toy dinosaur, plastic bug or spider, or another object into the clay. You can even use sticks and rocks to form a dinosaur foot! Carefully remove the object. The impression (the dent left behind by your object) is just like the impressions left behind by dinosaurs! Follow the instructions on the package for letting your clay harden.

Share the fossil cast you made with your den.

Date	Den Leader's OK

REQUIREMENT 3B | Make a dinosaur dig. Be a paleontologist, and dig through a dinosaur dig made by another member of your den. Show and explain the ways a paleontologist works carefully during a dig.

It's time to have a dinosaur dig! Paleontologists dig through layers of the ground to carefully uncover bones, rocks, leaf fossils, and other objects that were left behind when the dinosaurs died.

Today, you are going to make your own dino dig! Carefully follow the instructions of your den leader.

Materials

- Disposable aluminum pan
- Plaster of paris
- Safety glasses, dust mask
- Various objects (toy dinosaurs, polished rocks, silk leaves, etc.)

 Safety: Be sure to give adults lots of space while they get the mix ready. Adults should wear safety glasses and a mask to keep from breathing in the dust.

Instructions

1. Have an adult mix plaster of paris.
2. Have an adult help you pour enough plaster of paris to cover the bottom of each pan. Place a few objects in the bottom layer.
3. Have an adult help you pour another layer, and place more objects.
4. Repeat until the pan is full.
5. Set the pan aside to dry until the next den meeting.

Paleontologists use many different types of tools to dig out bones and fossils. Because they do not want to damage anything, they usually use small tools like chisels and paint brushes.

You will be digging through plaster instead of rock, so you can use a large nail, a small hammer, and paint brushes to dig out your objects.

Be careful while you work so you can get the dinosaurs out in one piece!

 Safety: For your safety, wear a mask and safety glasses while you work just in case any plaster pieces or dust go flying through the air.

Can you imagine how exciting it must be for a scientist to uncover bones that are millions of years old? Share with your den leader how your dinosaur dig went and what you found.

Date	**Den Leader's OK**

REQUIREMENT 4 | Make edible fossil layers. Explain how this snack is a good model for the formation of fossils.

Different types of soil, rock, and weather affected the way fossils formed. Sometimes an object was encased, or completely covered; sometimes it became soft and dissolved; and sometimes rock formed around it. To show fossil layers, we are going to make a display that you can eat!

Check with your den leader to find out if your den will do this activity as a group. If you would like to try it with your family, follow the directions below.

Materials

- Large, clear plastic cups
- Flavored gelatin
- Animal crackers
- Pudding
- Crushed graham crackers

Instructions

1. Scoop some crushed graham crackers onto the flavored gelatin layer.
2. Place an animal cracker on the layer.
3. Scoop more graham crackers on top, making sure to cover the animal cracker.
4. Scoop pudding onto the graham crackers.
5. Place an animal cracker on the layer.
6. Scoop more pudding.

While eating your fossil layer dessert, notice that some of the animal crackers stay crunchy and some are soft. This is because some of them will absorb moisture from their surrounding layers and some will not. Each of the materials surrounding the animal crackers affects them in a different way.

Now you can see how layers of the earth's crust covered over, surrounded, or even absorbed fossils. The reason that scientists rarely find a complete skeleton of a dinosaur is because some of the bones dissolved over time in the wet conditions of the soil they were in. Who knew fossil layers could be so tasty?

Date

Den Leader's OK

FINDING YOUR WAY

ELECTIVE ADVENTURE

Complete the following requirements.

1. Do the following:

    A. Using a map of your city or town, locate where you live.

    B. Draw a map for a friend so he or she can locate your home, a park, a school, or other locations in your neighborhood. Use symbols to show parks, buildings, trees, and water. You can invent your own symbols. Be sure to include a key so your symbols can be identified.

2. Do the following:

    A. Identify what a compass rose is and where it is on the map.

    B. Use a compass to identify which direction is north. Show how to determine which way is south, east, and west.

3. Go on a scavenger hunt using a compass, and locate an object with a compass.

4. Using a map and compass, go on a hike or walk with your den or family.

SNAPSHOT OF ADVENTURE

The ancient Greeks went on many adventures. Their writings told of faraway lands and treasures. To explain where their adventures took them, they created geography. Geography is the science of the earth's surface. *Ge* means "earth" and *grapho* means "to write."

Maps and compasses are tools that have helped travelers for hundreds of years know if they are headed in the right direction. In this adventure, you will learn to read maps and use one on a hike. You'll also get to make your own map and use a compass on a scavenger hunt. Just like the ancient Greek explorers, it's time for you to lead the way on another great adventure, Wolf!

COMPLETE THE FOLLOWING REQUIREMENTS.

REQUIREMENT 1 | Do the following:

REQUIREMENT 1A | Using a map of your city or town, locate where you live.

A map is a drawing or sketch of an area or country. Explorers have used maps since ancient times to travel from one place to another. We use maps every day. You may have used a map to locate a trail you hiked with your den or family.

Now it's time to get to know your town better and the area where you live!

Aerial view of Columbus, Georgia

You can find a map of your city or town at a public library, the local convention and visitors bureau, or the chamber of commerce.

You can also find a map of your area on the internet if you have permission from the adult working with you on this adventure. Some online map programs might allow you to see a satellite image of your street and zoom in on a picture of your home.

If you are online, you can find the location of your home by typing in your street address with an adult's help. Your home will not be pictured on a regular city or town map, though.

1A

_____   _____
Date   **Den Leader's OK**

Maps have lines, symbols, and colors. A key, or legend, tells you what those symbols and colors mean. Using the key, locate different symbols on the map. What symbols did you find?

Now make a map of your neighborhood. Include your home, your school, or other locations you choose. Make up your own symbols to show parks, buildings, and bodies of water nearby.

Be sure to mark the streets and landmarks on your map so a friend could easily find the location you selected.

1B

_____   _____
          Date   **Den Leader's OK**

REQUIREMENT 2A | Identify what a compass rose is and where it is on the map.

A compass rose is a figure on a compass, some maps, and nautical charts. It is used to show the four basic geographic directions: north, south, east, and west. This symbol has been used by mapmakers since ancient times.

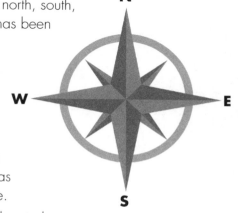

The term "rose" comes from the figure's compass points, which look a little like the petals of a rose. It was originally used to tell the direction of the winds and was sometimes called a wind rose.

The compass rose is often located in a bottom corner of a map. Reading a compass rose is a lot like reading a clock. You start at the top, which is where north is located.

Here's how to remember the points of a compass rose going clockwise in a circle: **Never Eat Soggy Waffles!**

Never = **North**

Eat = **East**

Soggy = **South**

Waffles = **West**

Look at the map above, and find the compass rose. Now point to a place located in the north on the map. Ask an adult to check—were you right? If you want to keep going, you can name places in the east, south, and west.

| Date | Den Leader's OK |

REQUIREMENT 2B | Use a compass to identify which direction is north. Show how to determine which way is south, east, and west.

North, south, east, and west are the points of a compass. A compass can help you figure out what direction is north. Once you know that, you can decide which direction to go to move toward your destination. You can also use a map and compass to figure out how to get from one place to another. Wherever you happen to be on earth, the compass needle will always point north.

Hold a compass flat in your hand. Look down at the needle to see where it is pointing. Turn your body slowly. Keep turning until the compass needle lines up with the north line or "N" on the grid.

Remember the floating needle is magnetized and the red end will always point to magnetic north. You can always figure out the other points of the compass when you stand facing north.

When you are facing north using a compass,

east will be on your right, south will be directly behind you, and west will be to your left. If you forget, remember "Never Eat Soggy Waffles" and you'll get right back on track.

2B

_____   _____
Date   **Den Leader's OK**

REQUIREMENT 3 | Go on a scavenger hunt using a compass, and locate an object with a compass.

It's time to have some fun using a compass! Your den leader or another adult will place an object or objects nearby for you to find. Then he or she will give you directions for using the compass to locate them.

First, find north on the compass and line up your body so you are facing north. The adult in charge will give you directions to an object from the position where you are standing.

Using the compass, follow the directions to get to the hidden object. Good luck on your scavenger hunt, Wolf!

Date   Den Leader's OK

You've practiced with your map and compass, and now you're ready to try out your skills on a hike. Plan a hike with your den or your family using a park map, a map of your community, or a map you have created.

Be sure to plan the route for your hike so you can follow the directions using your map. Remember to bring along a pack with the Cub Scout Six Essentials and dress for the weather.

When you get to a point on the map that is marked, such as the intersection of two streets or a marked fork in the trail, stop and orient yourself by using the map. Point to the place where you are on the map, and show an adult that you know your exact location.

Date	Den Leader's OK

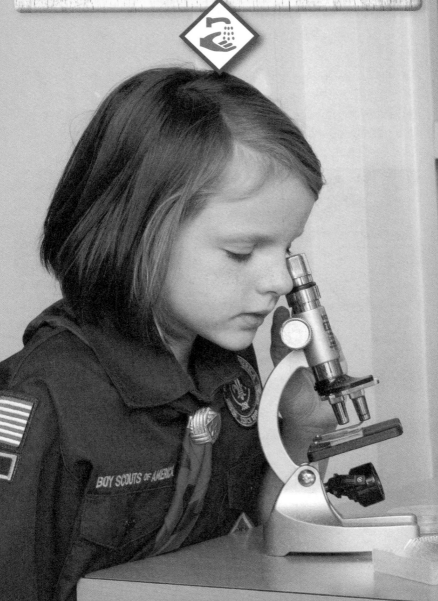

GERMS ALIVE!

ELECTIVE ADVENTURE

Complete at least five of the following requirements.

1. Wash your hands while singing the "Happy Birthday" song.
2. Play Germ Magnet with your den or your family. Wash your hands afterward.
3. Conduct the sneeze demonstration.
4. Conduct the mucus demonstration with your den or family.
5. Grow a mold culture. At a den or pack meeting, show what formed.
6. Make a clean room chart, and do your chores for at least one week.

SNAPSHOT OF ADVENTURE

In this adventure, you'll get to explore how to keep your body healthy. Why is it important to wash your hands? Why is the slimy mucus in your nose (yep, snot) important to your health? What happens if you sneeze into the air instead of the bend in your elbow? How does keeping your room clean help keep you healthy?  We will explore all of these questions while we journey through the yucky world of germs!

REQUIREMENT 1 | Wash your hands while singing the "Happy Birthday" song.

Have you washed your hands today? You probably get asked that question all the time by your teachers, parents, and other adults. So why is everyone all worked up about keeping your hands clean? Well, it turns out that washing your hands is the best way to keep germs from spreading.

Germs are all around us. They are so tiny you need a microscope to see them, but plants, animals, and people can still get sick from germs.

Four common kinds of germs are bacteria, fungi (FUNG-gahy), viruses, and protozoa (proh-TUH-zoh-uh).

- **Bacteria** are tiny germs that live inside and outside your body. The next time you get a sore throat or ear infection, bacteria may be the bad guys.

- **Fungi** live in moist, warm places and can cause itchy rashes and mold.

- **Viruses** get inside your body, spread quickly, and cause colds, flu, chicken pox, and lots of other illnesses.

- **Protozoa** live in water and cause intestinal infections.

You can see why you don't want these germs around! If you want to keep them away, the best place to start is with your hands. Hands are germ magnets. When we touch other people, those germs are passed from hand to hand.

You should wash your hands at these times:

- After you go to the bathroom
- After you play with a dog, cat, or other animal
- After you blow your nose or sneeze or cough
- After you touch garbage
- Before and after you help prepare food
- Before you set the table
- Before you eat
- Before you put away clean dishes
- When your hands have dirt on them

Here's how to get your Wolf paws perfectly clean:

1. Use water to wet your hands. 2. Use soap (any kind is fine).

3. Work the soap into a lather on both sides of your hands. Remember to wash your wrists, between your fingers, and around your fingernails, where many germs hide.

4. Wash for 10 to 15 seconds while singing the "Happy Birthday" song and then rinse off the soap. Don't stop washing your hands until you sing it twice!

_____   _____
Date   **Den Leader's OK**

Now that you have clean hands, let's find out just how far and how quickly germs spread! Play the Germ Magnet game with your den or family.

GERM MAGNET GAME

Instructions

1. Wash your hands, and form a circle with the group.

2. An adult will put a pinch of bright colored glitter into one person's hand in the circle. Have that person shake hands with the next person. Do not touch your face or eyes with glitter on your hands!

3. Pass the handshake around the circle and see how far the "germs" (glitter) go. You can also add a second color to show how different "germs" can build up.

4. Wash your hands after the game. Be sure to clean up all of the glitter with a vacuum cleaner or a broom and dustpan!

What did you learn about how germs are passed by hand contact? Did it help you understand why an important part of the Scout Law we live by is "A Scout is clean"? Share with your den leader what you learned while playing the game.

 A Scout is clean. As Scouts, we keep our minds and bodies fit and clean. We also help keep our homes, communities, and outdoor spaces clean. We do these things out of respect for others, the environment, and ourselves.

_____   _____
Date   Den Leader's OK

Sneezes sound funny, but they are actually a powerful tool your body uses to get rid of dust or other things that are irritating your body.

Sneezing can also spread germs quickly and powerfully. Because a Scout is courteous, always protect the people around you by sneezing into a tissue or the crook of your elbow.

You can conduct a sneeze demonstration to show why you should block a sneeze with your elbow. Because you can't see germs without a microscope, you will use some other items to show what happens when you sneeze.

Materials

- ◆ Blanket, old sheet, or tarp with circles drawn on it in the form of a bull's-eye. Each "ring" of the bull's-eye should be 12 inches apart.
- ◆ Balloon (check for latex allergies)
- ◆ Paper confetti
- ◆ Piece of paper to roll into a funnel
- ◆ Tape
- ◆ Tape measure

Symbols: The bull's-eye represents the air. The balloon is a sneeze. The confetti represents the germs.

Instructions

1. Roll the paper to make a funnel.

2. Insert the small end of the funnel into the balloon.

3. Pour a couple of tablespoons of paper confetti into the balloon.

4. Blow up the balloon to its full size and tie it.

 Safety: Pinch the balloon when you stop blowing so you don't get any confetti in your mouth.

5. Place the blanket with the bull's-eye on the ground.

6. Place the balloon in the center ring of the bull's-eye. Guess how far you think the "sneeze" will spread the "germs." Have the other members of the den move several feet away from the balloon.

7. On the count of three, yell, "ACHOO!" Pop the balloon.

How far did the confetti spread? Measure the distance the "sneeze" traveled with a tape measure. How did your guess compare to the results? How easy or hard would it be to catch a cold or other illness from a single sneeze?

Remember to clean up after your demonstration and dispose of the confetti and balloon properly.

_____   _____
Date   **Den Leader's OK**

Sometimes people call it "snot" or "boogers," but the proper name is "mucus." The slimy stuff inside of your nose has an important job to do. Mucus is a filter. Filters catch objects and make sure that they cannot go any farther.

Mucus catches tiny things in the air that you breathe in through your nose. These could be germs, dust particles, or pollen from plants. No matter what it is that your nose is breathing in, mucus catches it. This is why you should always use a tissue to blow your nose instead of picking it with your fingers.

You are going to make a bag of fake "mucus" and then see how it catches dust. You will also get to see a cool reaction when you mix the ingredients for your fake "mucus" together! A Scout is helpful, obedient, and courteous. Be sure to follow your den leader's or parent's instructions while doing this demonstration.

FAKE MUCUS RECIPE

Materials
- Borax
- Warm water
- White school glue
- Food coloring

- Two plastic containers
- Quart-size zippered storage bag
- Pinch of dirt, flour, glitter, or cocoa
- Paper plate

Container One
- 2 tablespoons borax
- 2 cups warm water

Container Two
- 2 teaspoons white glue
- 3 teaspoons warm water

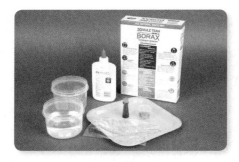

Instructions

1. Dissolve borax into the warm water in container one.

2. Dissolve glue into the warm water in container two.

3. Add a few drops of yellow or green food coloring to the container of glue, and mix.

4. Add one to two teaspoons of the borax mixture to the glue mixture. Begin stirring, and watch as the mixture starts to form into "slime."

After you make your fake mucus, play with it for a few minutes. What does it feel like? How do you think something so slimy could protect your body?

Now put your fake mucus on a paper plate. Place a pinch of dirt, glitter, flour, or cocoa in your hand and gently blow it onto the mucus. Did you notice how it stuck onto the surface? This is how the mucus in your nasal membrane inside your nose filters stuff. Examine the results, and describe what you learned to your parent or guardian or den leader.

Don't forget the final step: Wash your hands! This is something we should always do when we handle mucus ... fake or real!

_____   _____
Date   **Den Leader's OK**

There are different types of mold, and they can grow on many surfaces.

Molds produce and release millions of spores. The spores are small enough to be moved around by air, water, and insects. Some molds also produce toxic agents. Being around mold can make people sick. That is why having a clean home is important to the health of everyone in your family.

With an adult's help, try this mold investigation.

MOLD GROWTH

Materials

+ Banana
+ Small piece of bread
+ Paper plates
+ Rubber gloves
+ Small piece of cheese
+ Sandwich bags

Instructions

1. Place the peeled banana, cheese, and bread in separate sandwich bags on paper plates.

2. Lightly sprinkle each food with water. Leave a small opening to let some air in.

3. Label the foods with a note that they should not be eaten.

4. Observe the three foods daily.

Which food grew mold faster? Write down your findings for a week. If you can, take pictures to share with your den.

 Safety: Wear rubber gloves to dispose of the food and paper plates after one week. Have an adult help you clean the area, and wash your hands with soap and water.

What did you learn? Share your findings with your den. Remember to store food properly to stay healthy!

_____   _____
Date   **Den Leader's OK**

REQUIREMENT 6 | Make a clean room chart, and do your chores for at least one week.

Now that you know how bacteria and germs can grow, you can see why it's important to keep your room clean. This healthy habit will give you a healthy habitat.

It can be hard to know where to start when cleaning your room. Make a list of small jobs. Then put the list together in a chart. You can check off each job as you finish it. It feels good to see a completed chart!

CHORE CHART

CHORE LIST	Monday	Tuesday	Wednesday	Thursday	Friday	Saturday	Sunday
Make your bed							
Empty trash can							
Clean up your toys							
Put away clothes							

_____ _____
Date   **Den Leader's OK**

GROW SOMETHING

ELECTIVE ADVENTURE

Complete the following requirements.

1. Select a seed, and plant it in a small container. Care for it for 30 days. Take a picture or make a drawing of your plant once each week to share with your den or family.

2. Find out the growing zone for your area, and share the types of plants that will grow best in your zone.

3. Visit or research a botanical or community garden in your area, and learn about two of the plants that grow there. Share what you have learned with your den or family.

4. Complete one of the following:

   A. Make a terrarium.

   B. Using a seed tray, grow a garden inside your home. Keep a journal of its progress for 30 days. Share the results with your den or family.

   C. Grow a sweet potato plant in water. Keep a journal of its growth for two weeks. Share the information with your den or family.

SNAPSHOT OF ADVENTURE

How do plants and vegetables grow? It seems like magic—we prepare the soil, stick a seed in the ground, water it, and before you know it something is growing. Wow! Some plants can even grow in water instead of soil.

Gardening takes commitment and work, but it can be very rewarding. Learning to take care of things is the key. Sun, water, shade, and fertilizer are all things that are very important in helping plants grow. In this adventure, you can try your hand at growing living things and learn more about the plants that are native to your area.

 This elective is also part of the World Conservation Award. (See page 299.)

COMPLETE THE FOLLOWING REQUIREMENTS.

> **REQUIREMENT 1** | **Select a seed, and plant it in a small container. Care for it for 30 days. Take a picture or make a drawing of your plant once each week to share with your den or family.**

Many of the plants we see in our daily lives grew from a seed. The seed is put into soil, fertilized, watered, and given a place with some light. Before you know it, a plant is growing. As the plant grows, it may be taken from its container and put into the ground, if it is an outside plant, or put in a bigger container, if it is an inside plant.

Some plants grow quickly, while others take a long time. For example, radishes are ready to harvest in about a month, while beans take about two months and pumpkins and watermelons take about four to five months. An oak tree, on the other hand, can take years just to get as tall as a Wolf Scout.

Choose a seed, and try growing your own plant.

1. Make holes in the bottom of a paper cup so water can drain.

2. Add potting soil.

3. Place the seed in soil as the package recommends.

4. Water the plant, and let it drain in a sink.

5. Place it in a sunny window on a tray.

6. Keep the soil moist, and watch it grow!

How much did your plant grow in 30 days? Take a picture or make a drawing of the plant you grew and share it with your den.

_____   _____
Date   Den Leader's OK

Different plants require different care. Some plants like a lot of sun, and some like the shade. Some grow where it is cold, and others like the heat. Many like lots of water, but some, like cacti, don't need much water at all. Knowing your growing zone will help you decide what will grow well in your area.

KEY
1
2
3
4
5
6
7
8
9
10
11

Look at the back of seed packages before you buy them to find out if the plants will do well in your growing zone. The seed packets will also give you information about how often to water your plant, what kind of light it needs, and how far apart to plant the seeds.

Do some research at the library or on the internet, with an adult's permission. Find out what kinds of plants grow best in your zone.

_____   _____
Date   Den Leader's OK

REQUIREMENT 3 | Visit or research a botanical or community garden in your area, and learn about two of the plants that grow there. Share what you have learned with your den or family.

Botanical gardens are large gardens that are open to the public. They are full of plants and flowers, often from far away. Labels tell visitors the botanical (or formal scientific) name of plants and flowers. For example, the botanical name for daisy is *Bellis perennis*. Visitors can learn about the plants or just enjoy looking at them.

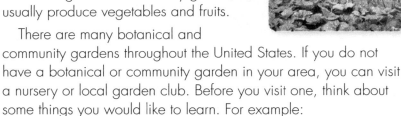

A community garden is a piece of public or private land gardened by a group of local people. People might share the work or have separate small plots of land to garden. Community gardens usually produce vegetables and fruits.

There are many botanical and community gardens throughout the United States. If you do not have a botanical or community garden in your area, you can visit a nursery or local garden club. Before you visit one, think about some things you would like to learn. For example:

♦ Which plants are easy to grow?

♦ How much light and water do different plants need?

♦ What other things do plants need to grow?

_____   _____
Date   Den Leader's OK

REQUIREMENT 4A | Make a terrarium.

When you create a terrarium, you build your own little world of plants inside a clear container. Terrariums look like aquariums, but they are made for plants instead of fish.

To make one, you can use a clear glass or plastic container with or without a lid. Choose a few plants for your terrarium that do well in the same kind of environment. You can plant small ferns, begonias, ivy, and moss together because they like the soil to be moist. For these plants, use a lid because they like humid air. If you see a lot of water droplets forming inside the container, remove the lid. Place the lid back on the terrarium once the droplets have evaporated.

You can also plant cactus and other succulents together because they need very little water. For these plants, do not place a lid on the container, as they need lots of air.

Materials

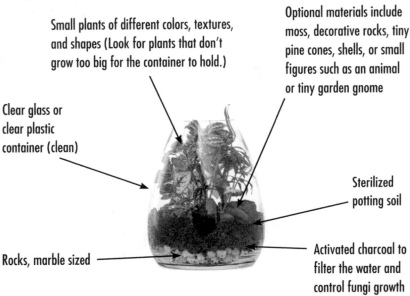

Small plants of different colors, textures, and shapes (Look for plants that don't grow too big for the container to hold.)

Optional materials include moss, decorative rocks, tiny pine cones, shells, or small figures such as an animal or tiny garden gnome

Clear glass or clear plastic container (clean)

Sterilized potting soil

Rocks, marble sized

Activated charcoal to filter the water and control fungi growth

Follow the picture to build your terrarium from the bottom up.

1. Place a 1-inch layer of rocks on the bottom.

2. Add a ½-inch layer of activated charcoal.

3. Fill the container half full of potting soil.

4. Plant small plants; leave space between them so they have room to grow.

5. Optional: Add decorative rocks, shells, or a small figure.

6. Water the plants a little, but not too much.

7. Place the terrarium in indirect light.

   Share the terrarium you made with your den.

Date　　　　　　　　**Den Leader's OK**

4A

REQUIREMENT 4B | Using a seed tray, grow a garden inside your home. Keep a journal of its progress for 30 days. Share the results with your den or family.

It's easy to start your garden inside your home in a seed tray.

Materials

- ◆ Plastic tray
- ◆ Potting soil
- ◆ Vegetable seeds

Instructions

1. Fill the tray half full with potting soil, and dampen.

2. Make lines across the soil for seed rows.

3. Place seeds in the rows. Leave space as directed.

4. Cover the seeds with a thin layer of soil.

5. Leave the tray where it is warm and light.

6. Keep the soil damp, and watch your indoor garden grow.

Every few days, take a close look at your seed tray and write down in your journal any changes you see. Before long, you should see seedlings pushing up out of the soil and leaves starting to grow. If you have an outdoor garden space and the weather is warm enough, you can plant the vegetables outside once they have grown to about 3 or 4 inches in height.

Date	Den Leader's OK

A plant does not always have to be in soil to grow. There are certain types of plants that will grow in water. Putting your plant in water will allow you to see the roots that will go deep in the ground once the plant is planted.

Materials
- Clear glass jar with a wide opening
- Wooden toothpicks
- Sweet potato

Instructions

1. Check that the sweet potato will fit in the jar with space around it. Push three or four toothpicks into the sweet potato to make a circle around the middle.

2. Rest the toothpicks on top of the jar. The upper half of the potato should be above the opening.

3. Fill the jar with enough water to cover the bottom half of the potato.

4. Place the jar in a window with plenty of sunlight.

5. Check the water regularly to be sure it covers half of the potato.

It will take two or three weeks to see any change in the potato. Then you will start to see roots growing from the potato's buds. The roots will reach down into the water. You will also see green leaves starting to grow from the top.

You can leave your potato in the jar, water it, and watch the vines grow longer, or you can replant it to a hanging basket in good soil when the leaves and roots have really started to grow. If you plant it in the ground in good soil, the sweet potato may spread and produce sweet potatoes that can be eaten!

Share the journal you kept of your plant's growth with your den.

_____   _____
Date   **Den Leader's OK**

HOMETOWN HEROES

ELECTIVE ADVENTURE

Complete the following requirements.

1. Talk with your family or den about what it means to you to be a hero. Share the name of someone you believe is a hero. Explain what it is that makes that person a hero.

2. Visit a community agency where you will find many heroes. While there, find out what they do. Share what you learned with your den.

3. With the help of a family member, interview one of your heroes, and share what you learn with your den. Tell why you think this person is a hero.

4. Complete one of the following:

   A. As a den or family, honor a service member by sending a care package along with a note thanking them for their service.

   B. With your family or den, find out about animals that are trained to help others in your community.

   C. Participate in or create an event that celebrates your hometown hero(es).

SNAPSHOT OF ADVENTURE

There are heroes all around us. A hero is someone we admire for being brave or good. Many heroes don't even think they are heroes. A hero takes care of people, helps others, and lives by beliefs like those in the Scout Oath and Scout Law. In fact, you will find many heroes who are part of Scouting. In this adventure, you will have the chance to learn about, talk to, and celebrate heroes in your hometown!

COMPLETE THE FOLLOWING REQUIREMENTS.

REQUIREMENT 1 | Talk with your family or den about what it means to you to be a hero. Share the name of someone you believe is a hero. Explain what it is that makes that person a hero.

There are many reasons a person is called a hero. Being brave, helping someone in need, and putting others first are some reasons people are called heroes. Police, firefighters, service members, doctors, and nurses are also thought of as heroes. Ordinary people can be heroes, too—even kids like you!

 A Scout is brave. One way to become brave is to learn about others who have done brave things.

Think about someone you believe is a hero. This could be someone you know or someone you have learned about. You could visit the library, or, with your parent's or guardian's permission, go online to learn more about the person. Find out what your hero did that was brave, caring, or special to help others. Share what you learn with your parent or guardian and your den.

_____   _____
Date   **Den Leader's OK**

Police officers and firefighters are trained to protect us from harm. They must be ready to risk their own lives to help others. Doctors and nurses are trained to take care of us, no matter how badly injured or sick we are. Service members are trained to protect our country from harm and to rescue their fellow soldiers in danger. There are many other places in your town where heroes work every day.

With your den or family, visit a place where people help others. Some choices are:

- ◆ EMT station
- ◆ Police or fire station
- ◆ School
- ◆ Veterans Affairs office
- ◆ Public health office
- ◆ Another community agency

Before you visit, write down some questions you would like to ask. Be sure to thank the people you meet for their service to your community and for taking the time to meet with you. Share what you learn with your den.

Date	Den Leader's OK

When you select a hometown hero to interview, think about people in your school, family, and community.

Here are some questions you might want to ask him or her.

1. What is your favorite part of your job?

2. What was your scariest or most difficult day on the job?

3. What keeps you coming back day after day?

4. How did you prepare for this job?

5. Who is *your* hero?

6. How does it make you feel to be able to help or protect others?

7. What qualities does a person need to do your job?

Be sure to end the interview by shaking hands and thanking your hero for serving the community. Share what you learned about your hometown hero with your den.

_____   _____
Date   Den Leader's OK

REQUIREMENT 4 | Complete one of the following:

REQUIREMENT 4A | As a den or family, honor a service member by sending a care package along with a note thanking them for their service.

Many service members might be away from home for the first time. A package from home with the things they love is a great way to lift their spirits and let them know that the people in their hometown care about them.

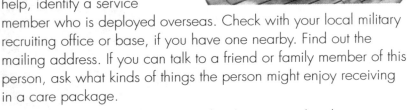

With your den leader's help, identify a service member who is deployed overseas. Check with your local military recruiting office or base, if you have one nearby. Find out the mailing address. If you can talk to a friend or family member of this person, ask what kinds of things the person might enjoy receiving in a care package.

Working with your den or your family, put together the care package. It might include favorite snacks, a magazine or good book, music, socks, sunscreen, candy, a game, and other fun things. Ask your den leader what you are allowed to send.

Write a note to include with your package, thanking the person for serving our country. Tell a little bit about yourself, and share some news from your hometown. Tell them you would really enjoy meeting them when they return from active duty and to stay safe.

4A

_____   _____
Date   **Den Leader's OK**

Animals can be heroes, too. Police dogs are trained to help police. These dogs can locate drugs, search for people who are lost, and help take criminals into custody.

Other service dogs and animals are trained to help people who are disabled or elderly.

Hearing dogs, or signal dogs, can be the ears of people who are deaf or hard of hearing. They can alert their owners to doorbells, oven timers, people calling their names, and other everyday sounds. They use a paw touch or nose bump to get their owners' attention. When they hear a fire alarm, these dogs are trained to take their owners outside.

Guide dogs help people who are blind or have low vision. They help people get around town on foot and with many other tasks.

Other service dogs help people with physical disabilities. They are trained to open doors, pull clothes off hangers, pick up dropped items, bring medications and the telephone, and do things that their owners cannot do on their own.

Remember, service animals are working. Ask permission before approaching a service animal.

Horses, cats, and other animals are also trained as therapy animals to bring cheer and provide stress relief to sick children, elderly people, and people with disabilities.

Find out about animals in your community that help people. You will be surprised how many animal heroes are living around you!

4B

Date   Den Leader's OK

REQUIREMENT 4C | Participate in or create an event that celebrates your hometown hero(es).

It is an honor to recognize those who are heroes. You and your den can find many opportunities to do just that.

Think about participating in an annual parade on Veterans Day or placing flags on service members' graves for Memorial Day. You may be able to take part in or help plan a neighborhood picnic to honor someone special in your community. Or you can help plan a homecoming celebration for someone from your town who has served overseas.

Work closely with your den to choose an event or to plan a way to honor someone. How did you feel honoring that person? Why are you proud to have them in your community? What have you learned about being a hero while you worked on this adventure?

_____   _____
Date   **Den Leader's OK**

MOTOR AWAY

ELECTIVE ADVENTURE

Complete the following requirements.

1. Do each of the following:

   A. Create and fly three different types of paper airplanes. Before launching them, record which one you believe will travel the farthest and what property of the plane leads you to make that prediction.

   B. Make a paper airplane catapult. Before launching a plane, record how far you believe it will travel and explain what information you used to make this prediction. After you make your prediction, launch the plane and measure how far it flies.

2. Make two different model boats and sail them. Choose different shapes for your boats.

3. Create a model car that moves under its own power.

SNAPSHOT OF ADVENTURE

There are many ways to make things go—electricity, fuel, and batteries, to name a few. Do you know that *you* have the power to make a boat sail in the water, make a spool car move forward, or make an airplane fly across the room?

Propulsion is what gives an object (such as a plane, car, or boat) the power to move. You will learn different ways to make and propel vehicles. Think about how the shapes of cars, boats, and planes affect the distance they can go. In this adventure, you will explore how you can use the air in your lungs, the strength of your Wolf paws, and the power of your imagination to make things go!

COMPLETE THE FOLLOWING REQUIREMENTS.

REQUIREMENT 1 | Do each of the following:

REQUIREMENT 1A | Create and fly three different types of paper airplanes. Before launching them, record which one you believe will travel the farthest and what property of the plane leads you to make that prediction.

Paper airplanes are light. This helps them fly through the air when you use the power in your muscles to propel them. But a real airplane is heavy. How does anything that big stay in the air?

Airplanes need to have lift to fly. Scientists explain lift with an idea called Bernoulli's (bur-NOO-leez) principle. As planes travel through the air, air travels over the wings. The shape of the wings makes the air travel faster over the top than beneath them. The difference in the air speeds creates higher pressure beneath the wings than above them. The pressure difference causes the wing to push upward, creating lift. The faster the plane moves through the air, the more air is forced under and over the wings, creating more lift.

Bernoulli's Principle

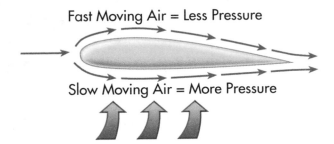

Fast Moving Air = Less Pressure

Slow Moving Air = More Pressure

To help understand how the principle works, try this with a sheet of paper:

Now it's time to make your own paper airplane. Choose one of the following plane designs or try your own design. See how different wing shapes change how the planes fly. Make careful, crisp folds to help your planes fly farther and faster.

ARROW

1. Place the paper as you see in the drawing. Fold the paper in half down the center, and unfold.

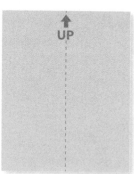

UP

2. Fold down each top corner so the edges line up along the center crease.

3. Fold each side over again to meet in the center. This will make a sharper point at the top of your plane.

4. Flip the paper over.

5. Fold the plane in half down the center. You should see the folds on the outside.

6. Starting 1 inch from the tip, make a crease straight to the back of the plane to create the wing. Repeat on the other side to match. Then lift the wings up so they are flat.

7. You might choose to cut two slits about 1 inch apart on each wing to create elevators. Angle the wings so you see a "V" from the front. This can make the plane more stable. Flip the elevator flaps up to make the plane rise. Flip them down to make the plane drop. Try flipping one elevator up to make the plane turn. Get ready for takeoff, Wolf!

Elevator Flaps

DELTA

1. Place the paper as you see in the drawing. Fold the paper in half down the center, and unfold. Now fold it in half in the other direction, and unfold. You should have four boxes from the creases.

2. Fold down the top corners so they meet in the center.

3. Fold the top edge down to the center.

4. Fold each top corner to the center along the crease running from top to bottom.

5. Fold the left side over the right side so the folds are hidden.

6. About 1 inch from the nose, start to fold down the wings in a straight line to the back of the plane. When both wings have been folded, lift them up to a slight "V" shape.

1.

2.

3.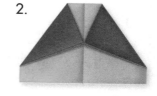

4.

5.

6.

DART

1. Place the paper as you see in the drawing. Fold the paper in half down the center, and unfold.

2. Fold down each top corner so the edges line up along the center crease.

3. Again, fold the outside edges to the center crease. This will create a sharper point at the top.

4.    **5.**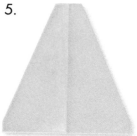

4. Fold down the point to the edge of the folded flaps.

5. Flip over your paper so the flat side is up.

6. Fold the plane in half.

6.

7. On one side, fold the tip in half at a slight angle. Make a crease to the back of the plane to create the wing. Repeat on the other side. You can add elevators, if you choose (see page 261).

You are ready to fly!

7.

Before you fly your three planes, guess how far each will go. Measure the distance after each first flight and see how close you came to guessing the distance each plane traveled. Share the results with your den.

_____   _____
Date   **Den Leader's OK**

Have you ever seen pictures of a fighter jet being launched from an aircraft carrier? Because the ship has a short runway, the flight deck crew hooks the jet to a catapult to fling it into the sky.

In the last requirement, you used your arm to thrust the plane forward. This time, a rubber band will propel the plane. Stretching the rubber band backward creates tension.

Because the material in a rubber band will return to its original size when you let go of it, the tension throws the plane forward as the rubber band shrinks. Listen carefully as your den leader or parent or guardian explains the safety rules for you to follow. Stay safe and have fun, Wolf!

Note to Parents and Other Caring Adults

To make sure every Wolf stays safe while items are being launched:

1. Check the rubber bands to be sure they are in good shape.
2. Consider putting a tape line around the launch area.
3. Use a countdown to signal when the Wolves need to leave the launch area.

PAPER AIRPLANE CATAPULT

Materials

- Paper airplane
- Hole punch or scissors
- Rubber band
- Tape measure
- Pencil

Instructions

1. Using one of the paper airplanes you made for requirement 1A, punch a hole through the underside of the paper airplane. If you are using scissors, have an adult carefully make a hole for you.

2. Use a pencil to thread the rubber band through the hole.

3. Tie the rubber band to the plane as shown.

4. Write down how far you think your plane will travel.

5. Find an open space outside. Never point the plane toward a person! Make sure no one is near your launch area so everyone stays safe and has fun.

6. Loop the rubber band over your thumb. Hold the back underside of the plane firmly. Pull back on the plane to stretch the rubber band. Let go of the plane, and watch it soar!

7. Measure the distance the plane traveled with a tape measure.

My prediction: _____

Actual distance: _____

How far did your plane go? Share your findings with your den.

1B

_____   _____
Date   **Den Leader's OK**

There are many kinds of boats. Some have motors. Some have sails. Some carry cargo. Some carry people. Some go fast, and some go slow.

The shape of the boat depends on the job it is supposed to do.

BUOYANCY

The buoyancy of an object measures whether it will float in water. Why is it that some objects float and some sink? You probably know from playing with objects in the water that a block of metal will sink and a piece of wood will float.

You also know that many large boats are made out of metal and they float. What makes this happen?

Whatever the boat is made from, it takes up space in the water. The amount of space it takes up is called displacement. If the amount of water the boat displaces weighs the same as the boat, the boat will float. You can try this by making a boat out of aluminum foil. Try different shapes to see which one holds the most cargo. You can use 1-cent coins to see what shape holds the most.

WHAT MAKES BOATS MOVE

Some boats use sails, and other boats use motors. Still others are moved through the water by using paddles.

The hull, or body, of the boat is important, too. Boats made to handle rough water have V-shaped hulls. Boats made for calm water or to carry heavy loads often have flat hulls.

Note to Parents and Other Caring Adults

For safety reasons, choose a small wading pool or other shallow container of water for floating the boats. Do not leave Scouts alone near the water. Place an adult in charge of that area. Do not use a swimming pool, pond, river, or lake to float the boats.

BUILD A BOAT

You might want to look around your house for things to use to build your boats. Use the facts about boats to help you make a model boat that works like a real boat. For different types of boats, you could use a water bottle, a milk carton cut in half lengthwise, an egg carton, corks stuck together with toothpicks or wrapped with rubber bands, or part of a pool noodle.

Your boat could be long or short, round or streamlined. For a round boat, you could recycle a yogurt container or a sour cream tub. For the mast, you could use a straw, a craft stick, or a stick from outside. For the sail, you could use a piece of paper or a piece of craft foam. Each choice you make will affect the way your boat moves.

Move your boats in the water by blowing air on the sails. While sailing your boats, notice how they are similar and how they are different. Talk about what you learned with your den.

What kind of boats did you make? How did they move in the water? Which shape worked best? Was one design better than another to propel the boat forward? Share what you learned with your den.

Date	Den Leader's OK

There are many ways to make a car that moves. A balloon-propelled car or spool car requires the power in you to create the momentum. Momentum is the force and strength of something when it moves. When you blow up the balloon or wind the rubber band and let go, the car moves. Here are a couple of ideas you might try.

BALLOON CAR

Materials
- ◆ Pint milk carton, cleaned
- ◆ Balloon
- ◆ Two straws
- ◆ Four spools
- ◆ Two skewers

Instructions
1. Cut one straw to create two pieces the same size as the side of the carton.

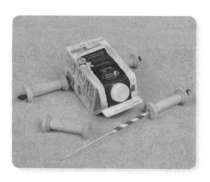

2. Slide one skewer through each straw. Slide a spool on each end, then tape the ends to hold the spools in place.

3. Lay the straws across the carton, and tape them in place. Check that the skewers can turn freely.

4. Slide the other straw into the balloon. Tape the end of the balloon to the straw so no air will escape.

5. Turn the carton over. Tape the straw with the balloon to the top of the balloon car.

6. Blow up the balloon, but don't tie the end. Now let go, and watch your car take off!

SPOOL CAR

Materials
- Spool
- Rubber band
- Two washers
- Two paper clips
- Tape
- Pencil

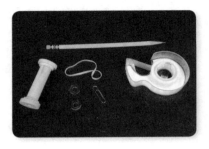

Instructions

1. Unfold one paper clip. Use it to push the rubber band through the hole in the spool until the rubber band goes all the way through.

2. Put the other paper clip through one end of the rubber band, and tape it to the end of the spool.

3. On the other end of the spool, thread two washers through the end of the rubber band. Then stick a pencil through the loop in the rubber band.

4. Hold the spool in one hand while you turn the pencil around and around in a clockwise direction to wind the rubber band tightly.

5. Put the spool on a flat surface and watch it go!

Test your balloon car or spool car on a carpeted surface, a smooth floor, a sidewalk, and the grass. How does your car work on each of these surfaces? What happens when you blow up the balloon only part of the way? Does the car go as far? What happens when you don't wind the rubber band tightly on the spool car? How far did your car travel? Share what you learned with your den.

_____ _____

Date   **Den Leader's OK**

PAWS OF SKILL

ELECTIVE ADVENTURE

Complete at least requirements 1-4. Requirements 5-7 are optional.

1. Talk with your family or den about what it means to be physically fit. Share ideas of what you can do to stay in shape.

2. With your family or den, talk about why it is important to stretch before and after exercising. Demonstrate proper warm-up movements and stretches before and after each activity you do that involves action.

3. Select at least two physical fitness skills and practice them daily for two weeks. See if you can improve during that time.

4. With your family or your den, talk about what it means to be a member of a team. Working together, make a list of team sports, and talk about how the team works together to be successful. Choose one and play for 30 minutes.

5. With your den, develop an obstacle course that involves five different movements. Run the course two times and see if your time improves.

6. With your den, talk about sportsmanship and what it means to be a good sport while playing a game or sport. Share with your den how you were a good sport or demonstrated good sportsmanship in requirement 4.

7. Visit a sporting event with your family or your den. Look for ways the team works together. Share your visit with your den.

SNAPSHOT OF ADVENTURE

Sports and active games are a great way to have fun and be healthy. You can also learn a lot about life playing them. Sports teach you to work with a team, help others, and follow rules. You can use the Scout Oath and Scout Law as guides when you are playing games and sports. In this adventure, you'll be challenged to exercise, play a team sport with your den, run an obstacle course, and show how to be a good sport. Time to move your powerful paws, Wolf!

**COMPLETE AT LEAST REQUIREMENTS 1–4.
REQUIREMENTS 5–7 ARE OPTIONAL.**

REQUIREMENT 1 | Talk with your family or den about what it means to be physically fit. Share ideas of what you can do to stay in shape.

What does it mean to be physically fit? Physically fit people have healthy hearts, lungs, and muscles they have developed from exercise. They don't get tired easily. They have a healthy weight. They are flexible so they move easily. Because they eat the right foods and exercise regularly, their bodies can fight off sickness better.

Eating a low-fat diet of vegetables, fruits, protein, and grains and limiting sugary foods is also important to help your body have energy to burn and build strong muscles.

Running, riding a bike, swimming, walking, and playing team sports are just a few ways you can stay fit. You should try to be active at least three times a week for 30 minutes each time. The trick is to do something you like and just get moving!

Now think about what you eat, how often you exercise, and the types of exercises you do. What can you do to be more fit? Share ideas with your den about what you can do to stay in shape.

Some exercises help build muscles.

Some exercises help improve your heart and lungs.

Date   Den Leader's OK

Stretching can warm you up before exercising or cool you down after.

A 10-minute warm-up will get your heart ready for activity. It will also loosen your muscles and help keep you from being injured.

After you exercise, spend about 5–10 minutes cooling down. These slow exercises help slow down your heart rate, keep your muscles from getting sore, and improve your flexibility.

Here are some warm-up and cool-down stretches you can try:

Take time to warm up and cool down each time you exercise. Demonstrate the warm-up and cool-down exercises you do to Akela or your den leader.

Date	Den Leader's OK

REQUIREMENT 3 | Select at least two physical fitness skills and practice them daily for two weeks. See if you can improve during that time.

You can't exercise just one time to become fit. When you practice your fitness skills many times, you will get better at doing them. Over time, you will be able to do more of each skill.

Choose two physical fitness skills, and practice them every day. Skills can include jumping jacks, sit-ups, pull-ups, or running in place.

1. Jumping jacks

2. Sit-ups

3. Pull-ups

4. Running in place

See if you are able to do more of each skill after practicing for two weeks. Remember to warm up before you begin and cool down when you are done.

Write down the skills you performed in the chart below. Write the number of each skill you were able to do at the start, after one week, and after two weeks.

Skill	Start	After Week 1	After Week 2
1. _____	_____	_____	_____
2. _____	_____	_____	_____
3. _____	_____	_____	_____
4. _____	_____	_____	_____

Share what skills you did and how you improved with your parent or guardian or your den leader.

_____   _____
Date   **Den Leader's OK**

REQUIREMENT 4 | With your family or your den, talk about what it means to be a member of a team. Working together, make a list of team sports, and talk about how the team works together to be successful. Choose one and play for 30 minutes.

When you play a sport by yourself, you can practice and improve on your own.

When you are part of a team, you need to work with others to get better. One player can't do everything. Each member helps the team in some way.

Make a list of team sports with your family or den. Think of ways a team works together to be successful. Choose one team sport to play for 30 minutes.

We chose: _____

In Scouting, you have already learned a lot about the importance of teamwork. Remember to support your teammates and play by the rules. Also be sure to treat coaches, other players, and referees with respect.

How did your team work together? How did you help your team?

_____   _____
Date   Den Leader's OK

Obstacle courses combine many activities. You get to move in different ways and try new skills. Like other sports activities, you can improve your time on an obstacle course with practice.

Work with your den to choose and create five activities. Here are some ideas:

- Crawling under a table or bench
- Jumping over soft pool noodles
- Tossing a ball or beanbag into a bucket
- Running through a sprinkler
- Weaving through cones
- Walking backward for 10 steps
- Balancing as you run along a snaky garden hose

What part of the course was easy for you? Was any part of the course difficult? Were you able to improve your time? Just as you pitched in to help your den build the course, be sure to help break it down afterward.

_____   _____
Date   **Den Leader's OK**

REQUIREMENT 6 | With your den, talk about sportsmanship and what it means to be a good sport while playing a game or a sport. Share with your den how you were a good sport or demonstrated good sportsmanship in requirement 4.

It is important to be a good sport while playing sports and games.

Here are some tips for showing good sportsmanship:

1. Play by the rules.
2. Be courteous to everyone.
3. Cheer for good plays.
4. Try your best.
5. Play to have fun.
6. Shake hands after the game.

 A Scout is helpful. You make a difference to your team when you are helpful—both on and off the field.

Share with your den how you practiced good sportsmanship when you played a team sport.

Date   **Den Leader's OK**

With your family or den, attend a sporting event. Your den can agree on a sport that is in season near you. The players might be in high school or college, or they might be professional players.

See if you can find out some information about the players and the team before you go. It also helps to understand the rules of the game before you watch a sporting event. It's more fun to watch if you know something about the team and how the game is played.

Tell your den about the ways you saw team members work together and how they showed sportsmanship.

_____   _____
Date   **Den Leader's OK**

SPIRIT OF THE WATER

H20

ELECTIVE ADVENTURE

Complete the following requirements.

1. Discuss how the water in your community can become polluted.

2. Explain one way that you can help conserve water in your home.

3. Explain to your den leader why swimming is good exercise.

4. Explain the safety rules that you need to follow before participating in swimming or boating.

5. Visit a local pool or public swimming area with your family or den. With qualified supervision, jump into water that is at least chest-high, and swim 25 feet or more.

SNAPSHOT OF ADVENTURE

Can you guess the answer to this riddle?

I can be a solid, liquid, or gas. I am two-thirds of your brain, and I can also be two-thirds of a tree. I existed during the days when dinosaurs were wandering around the earth and I have not changed. What am I?

If you guessed water, you are right!

Water is an important force in our lives. It can be as gentle as a spring sun shower or as powerful as a hurricane. All living things need water to live, but we use water for more than just survival. We use it for fun, too! In this adventure, you will learn how to conserve water, how to keep yourself safe in the water, how to become a better swimmer, and how to have a great time splashing around.

REQUIREMENT 1 | Discuss how the water in your community can become polluted.

Most communities have a way to get clean drinking water. Water comes from lakes, rivers, or wells tapped into an underground water source called an aquifer. The water is filtered, and then it travels through a maze of pipes to your faucet. With help from an adult, find out where the drinking water in your community comes from.

Human activity pollutes water. Water is polluted when it becomes spoiled by chemicals, waste, trash, or other particles. Polluted water can become harmful to people, fish, and animals that need fresh water to survive.

The water molecules that were on the earth when dinosaurs lived are the same water molecules that are around today. So when we pollute water today, that same water will stay in the environment.

Here are some of the sources of water pollution:

SOME CAUSES OF WATER POLLUTION

Hazardous
chemicals

Soaps and
detergents

Trash and litter

Oil and other
chemicals

Air pollution
from cars

Pesticides and
fertilizers

 A Scout is loyal. Taking care of the water in your community is a way to show loyalty.

WATER POLLUTION DEMONSTRATION

This activity will show you how quickly pollution can spread through groundwater.

Materials

- Clear glass loaf pan or baking pan
- Powdered drink mix (red or purple in color)
- Sand
- Spray bottle filled with water
- Book or small block of wood

Instructions

1. Make a small pile of powdered drink mix in one end of the clear glass pan.

2. Sprinkle sand over the rest of the pan.

3. Place the end of the pan with the powdered drink mix on top of the book or wood block so the pan is tilted.

4. Using the spray bottle of water, wet the sand. (Make sure it's really wet.) Let it sit for a few minutes, and then wet it again.

5. Carefully lift up the pan and look underneath it. What is happening?

As you can see, the water is carrying the powdered drink mix through the pan. Pollutants spread through our sources of water the same way. They can travel a long distance and can damage drinking water miles from where the pollution starts!

Think about how water is used in your community and how it might be polluted. Share what you learned about water pollution in your community with your den.

_____   _____
Date   **Den Leader's OK**

REQUIREMENT 2 | Explain one way that you can help conserve water in your home.

Water is very important to our survival and the survival of our planet. It is up to all of us to help conserve it, not waste it. For this requirement, you will have to explain how you can save water in your home. To help you, think about the ways your family uses water to do the following activities:

- Brushing teeth
- Bathing
- Washing dishes
- Watering the grass or plants
- Cooking food

Look at your family's current water bill or find out how many gallons the average household in your community uses in a month. How many gallons of water per month does your family use? Find a gallon-size container to help you picture the amounts. Now, think about how you could use less water. For example:

- Turn off the tap while you brush your teeth. Turn it back on to rinse your mouth. You could save up to 8 gallons of water a day and 200 gallons each month! That's enough to fill a large fish tank!

• If you wash dishes by hand, do not let the water run when you're not rinsing the dishes. You can save up to 200 gallons of water a month.

• Take five-minute showers. Short showers use much less water than filling a bathtub.

• Make sure you turn off the faucet completely each time you use it, and fix faucet leaks. A little drip can waste hundreds of gallons of water.

• Water your yard early in the morning or in the evening, so that the water does not evaporate quickly in the heat of the day. Check to see if your community has other rules or restrictions on watering lawns.

• Wash your bike or your family's car with a bucket of water. If you use a hose, do not let it run the whole time.

Share with your den one way you will save water at home, and make saving water a good habit!

2

_____ _____
Date   **Den Leader's OK**

REQUIREMENT 3 | Explain to your den leader why swimming is good exercise.

Swimming is a fun way to help you stay fit and healthy. Because water is about 12 times as dense, or thick, as air, you must work harder to move in the water. This helps your muscles get stronger.

Your lungs and heart also become stronger when you swim. Swimming helps your heart provide better blood flow throughout your body.

For people who are injured or disabled, swimming is often a safe way to exercise. Your body does not need to support all of its  weight in the water, so swimming puts less stress on an injury.

Talk to your den leader about why swimming is good exercise.

3

_____ _____
Date   **Den Leader's OK**

Let's get ready to swim! Start by learning how to stay safe around the water.

When you were a Tiger, you learned the SCOUT water safety chant. Use it when you go swimming or boating.

> **S** is Someone's **watching. Never swim alone.**
>
> **C** is Check **the rules. Know where you can roam.**
>
> **O** is Only **buddies should go from the shore.**
>
> **U** is know what "U" can do. Don't do any more.
>
> **T** is Tell **a grown-up if someone is in need.**
>
> SCOUT **shows safety. Now you take the lead!**

When going on a Scouting adventure, always stay with your buddy, even when in the water. You and your buddy will swim together and will be there for each other in case something happens. Remember that the buddy system makes swimming safer.

When you swim with your den, there will be a buddy check. When you hear "buddy check," stop where you are, join and raise hands with your buddy, and wait quietly.

Leaders will count pairs to make sure everyone is safe and with their buddy.

adult supervision

life jacket

6

For this adventure, demonstrate the buddy check and repeat the SCOUT safety chant for your den leader or Akela.

You also need to know how to stay safe when you go boating. Remember:

♦ Only go boating with adult supervision.

♦ Always wear a life jacket when you go boating.

♦ A balanced boat will help keep the boat from tipping over.

When you go boating, always follow the safe boating rules explained by your leader or lifeguard. Explain what you've learned about safe boating to your den leader.

Date _____ **Den Leader's OK** _____

REQUIREMENT 5 | **Visit a local pool or public swimming area with your family or den. With qualified supervision, jump into water that is at least chest-high, and swim 25 feet or more.**

Now it's time to try some new skills at the pool.

First, practice blowing bubbles out of your nose in the water. This skill will keep the water from going up your nose when you jump in. Then learn how to safely jump feet first into water. The best way to jump is with your arms forward and legs slightly apart, one in front of the other. Lifeguards, scuba divers, and Scouts like you enter the water this way to avoid dangers beneath the water.

Once you are in the water, do your best to swim at least 25 feet. Swimming is a lot like other sports: When you practice it, you get better and faster. One stroke you can use is the front crawl. To do the front crawl, lie on your stomach in the water, kick your feet behind you, and paddle forward with your arms. If you are unsure how to do a front crawl, ask an adult for help.

<table>
<tr><td>_____</td><td>_____</td></tr>
<tr><td>Date</td><td>Den Leader's OK</td></tr>
</table>

SPECIAL AWARDS YOU CAN EARN

The following awards can be earned while you are a Cub Scout. Check with your pack leaders or go to **www.scouting.org** (with a parent's or guardian's permission) to learn more.

Conservation Good Turn Award

The Conservation Good Turn is an award packs may earn by partnering with a conservation or environmental organization to choose and carry out a Good Turn in their home communities.

Outdoor Activity Award

Tiger, Wolf, Bear, and Webelos Scouts have the opportunity to earn the Cub Scout Outdoor Activity Award. Scouts may earn the award in each of the program years as long as the requirements are completed again each year. Cub Scouts complete specific requirements for each rank, including a number of different outdoor activities.

National Summertime Pack Award

The National Summertime Pack Award encourages packs to be active when school is out for the summer. Youth and adult pack members can earn the award by taking part in one activity per month in June, July, and August.

Emergency Preparedness Award

Cub Scouts who want to take steps to prepare themselves and their families in case of an emergency may earn the Emergency Preparedness Award. Cub Scouts may earn the award at each rank for completing increasingly challenging requirements.

STEM/Nova Awards

The Nova awards for Cub Scouts are for Wolf, Bear, and Webelos Scouts who are interested in learning more about science, technology, engineering, and mathematics. These awards may not be earned by Lion or Tiger Scouts.

For their first Nova awards, Scouts have the opportunity to earn the Nova award patch, followed by three more π pin-on devices. The patch and the three devices represent each of the four STEM topics. The Supernova awards have more challenging requirements and recognize more in-depth, advanced achievement in STEM-related activities.

World Conservation Award

The World Conservation Award for Cub Scouts provides an opportunity for individual Wolf, Bear, and Webelos Scouts to "think globally" and "act locally" to preserve and improve our environment. This program is designed to make youth members aware that all nations are closely related through natural resources, and that we are interdependent with our world environment.

Requirements for this award must be completed *in addition to* any similar requirements completed for rank. This award may not be earned by Lion or Tiger Scouts.

Bobcat Trail

Your name _____

Fill in seven tracks to earn the Bobcat badge.

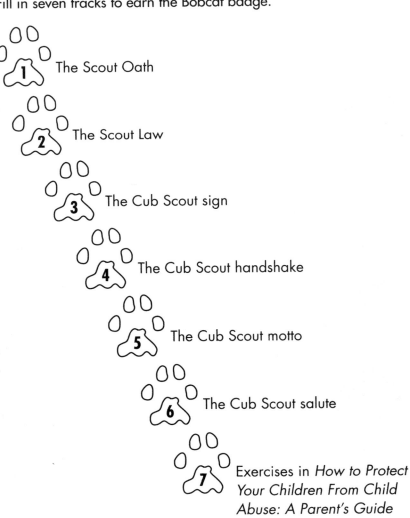

1. The Scout Oath

2. The Scout Law

3. The Cub Scout sign

4. The Cub Scout handshake

5. The Cub Scout motto

6. The Cub Scout salute

7. Exercises in *How to Protect Your Children From Child Abuse: A Parent's Guide*

Wolf Adventure Tracking

Call of the Wild
Do 1–4 and ONE other

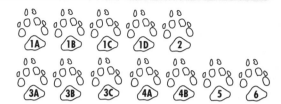

(1A) (1B) (1C) (1D) (2)
(3A) (3B) (3C) (4A) (4B) (5) (6)

**Council Fire
(Duty to Country)**
Do 1 and 2 and ONE other

(1) (2) (3) (4) (5) (6) (7)

Duty to God Footsteps
Do 1 OR 2 and TWO others

(1) (2) (3) (4) (5) (6)

Howling at the Moon
Complete all

(1) (2) (3) (4)

Paws on the Path
Do 1–5; 6 and 7
are optional

(1) (2) (3) (4) (5) (6) (7)

Running With the Pack
Complete all

(1) (2) (3) (4) (5) (6)

Elective _____

Youth Protection
Same as Bobcat No. 7

     **Cyber Chip**

Elective Adventures

Adventures in Coins
Do 1-4; 5-7 are optional

(1) (2) (3) (4) (5) (6) (7)

Air of the Wolf
Complete all

Do TWO of these: (1A) (1B) (1C) (1D)

Do TWO of these: (2A) (2B) (2C) (2D) (2E)

Code of the Wolf
Complete all

Do TWO of these: (1A) (1B) (1C) (1D) (1E)

Do ONE of these: (2A) (2B) (2C)

Do ONE of these: (3A) (3B) (3C)

Do ONE of these: (4A) (4B) (4C)

Collections and Hobbies
Complete all

(1) (2)

Do ONE of these: (3A) (3B)

Do ONE of these: (4A) (4B)

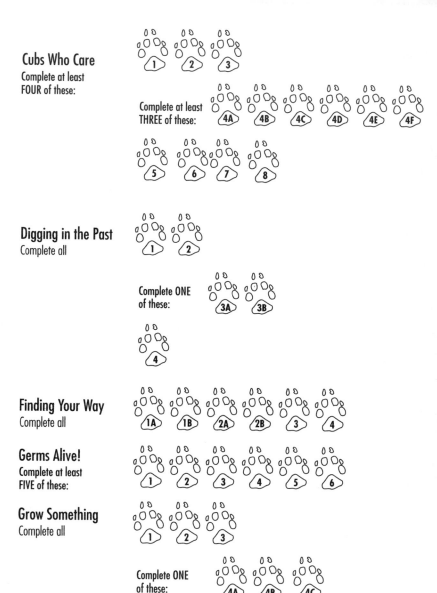

Cubs Who Care
Complete at least
FOUR of these:

Complete at least
THREE of these:

Digging in the Past
Complete all

Complete ONE
of these:

Finding Your Way
Complete all

Germs Alive!
Complete at least
FIVE of these:

Grow Something
Complete all

Complete ONE
of these:

Hometown Heroes
Complete all

①　②　③

Complete ONE of these:

④A　④B　④C

Motor Away
Complete all

①A　①B　②　③

Paws of Skill
Complete at least 1–4;
5–7 are optional

①　②　③　④　⑤　⑥　⑦

Spirit of the Water
Complete all

①　②　③　④　⑤

Acknowledgments

The Boy Scouts of America gratefully acknowledges the contributions of the many Cub Scouts, Scouters, subject experts, and staff throughout the nation for their help in preparing the *Wolf Handbook*. A special thank-you to the Cub Scout Handbook Task Force for their leadership: national Cub Scout chair, Lucia Cronin; task force committee; Linda Baker, Steve Bowen, Silvia de la Cruz, and Michelle Holmes; and national director, Cub Scouting, Anthony Berger.

Photo/Illustration Credits

Illustration

ChooseMyPlate.gov—page 104

Jeff Ebbeler—pages 157 and 159

Benjamin Eggleston—page 66

Aleksey Ivanov—pages 233 and 289

John McDearmon—page 8 and inside back cover

Grant Miehm—page 248 ("Scouts in Action" comic)

Shutterstock.com, courtesy—pages 46 (*flag*, ©Naypong), 192 (©Elenarts), 193 (*Apatosaurus*, ©Catmando), 194 (*Triceratops*, ©3Dalia; *Anklyosaurus*, ©Archie MKDesign; *Parasaurolophus*, ©Jean Michel Gerard), 195 (*Tyrannosarus rex*, ©leonello calvetti; *Spinosaurus*, ©Valentyna Chukhlyebova), 196 (*Velociraptor*, ©3Dalia), 197 (*Archaeopteryx*, ©leonello calvetti; *Pteranodon*, ©Catmando), 199 (©Computer Earth), 213 (©Zmiter), and 214 (©deer boy).

Rob Schuster—pages 38–40, 47, 53, 90–91, 127, 161, 239 (*planting zone map*), 258, 259 (*paper airplanes*), and 260–264

N. Tamura/CC-BY-SA-3.0—page 196 (*Hesperornithiformes*)

Photography

AXIS Dance Company, Courtesy. Dancers: Joel Brown & Sebastian Grubb. In choreography by Amy Seiwert. Photo by David DeSilva. 2012—page 189

BSA—pages 56 and 293

David Carlson—pages 286, 292 (*girl watering lawn*), 294, and 296

Tom Copeland—pages 12 (*marsh*), 175, 250, 284, 291, 292 (*girl with bicycle*), and 295

Jean Driscoll, courtesy—page 187 (*Jean Driscoll*)

Caroline Finnegan—pages 120–121, 230, 244, 245 (*sweet potatoes in water*), and 290

Elias Goldensky, Library of Congress Prints and Photographs Division—page 187 (*Franklin Roosevelt*)

Google Maps—211

Library of Congress, Prints and Photographs Division—pages 51, 52 *(Salt Lake City, 1904)*, 63, and 187 *(Thomas Edison)*

Whitman Studio, Library of Congress Prints and Photographs Division—page 188 *(Helen Keller)*

Spencer G. Lucas, Ph.D., courtesy—page 201

Roger Morgan—pages 73, 172, and 282

NASA.gov—page 188 *(Stephen Hawking)*

Brian Payne—pages 12 *(forest)*, 234, 256, 268 *(boats)*, and 277 *(boy running)*

Randy Piland—pages 17, 19 *(girl)*, 24, 26, 31–32, 48, 50, 55, 59, 64, 72, 94–95, 97, 101, 106, 135, 140–141, 142, 158, 168, 173, 176, 182, 184–185, 206, 210, 212, 215, 219, 236 *(people in garden)*, 239 *(seed packets)*, 243, 246, and 277 *(boy with weights)*

Michael Roytek—pages 1–2, 4–7, 14, 18, 19 *(boy)*, 27, 37, 44, 46 *(Scouts)*, 54, 61, 68 *(Scouts)*, 70, 74, 76, 79–81, 83–84, 88 *(boy with binoculars)*, 92, 98–99, 100, 102–103, 113, 124, 128–129, 133–134, 136–138, 146 *(girls playing game)*, 147, 149–151, 160, 162, 164, 166, 178, 186, 190, 202–203, 208, 216–218, 221–229, 237–238, 251–252, 255, 257, 259 *(Scout)*, 266–267, 268 *(single boat)*, 269, 270–274, 278–279, 292 *(boys washing dishes, Scout washing hands)*, and 297

Shutterstock.com, courtesy—pages 11 (©Panachai Cherdchucheep), 28 *(background, ©BrAt82; compass, ©GOLFX)*, 30 (©Maridav), 41 *(chipmunk, ©Wildphoto3; butterfly, ©Mrsirap)*, 42 *(turtle, ©Paul Reeves Photography; bird, ©Steve Byland)*, 52 *(present-day Salt Lake City, ©Andrew Zarivny)*, 58 *(church, ©almondd; synagogue, Irnya Liveoak; mosque, Roman Yanusnevsky)*, 65 (©Delmas Lehman), 68 *(stars, ©Nicemonkey)*, 69 (©Ronnie Howard), 82 (©tkemot), 88 *(hawk, ©Robert L. Kohthenbeutel)*, 89 *(deer, ©David Byron Keener)*, 108 (©Ethan Daniels), 111 *(minting machine, ©s spopov)*, 112 *(Denver mint, ©Henryk Sadura)*, 130 *(basketball, ©Aaron Amat; pump, ©Deslife)*, 132 (©Beata Becia), 146 *(clothespins, ©timquo)*, 152 *(fern, ©Vaclav Volrab; bees, ©Studio Smart)*, 153 *(arched bridge, ©Israel Hervas Bengochea; beamed bridge, ©Toa55; suspension bridge, ©f11photo)*, 155 (©Wolfgang Zwanzger), 167 (©Anna Biancoloto), 169 (©Denemmanuel), 170 (©Caruso Christian), 174 *(background, ©Oksana Boguslavska)*, 180–181 (©mezzotintl), 198 (©Jane Rix), 204 (©stockphoto mania), 205 *(sandstone, ©alysta; crackers, ©Danny Smythe)*, 235 (©KPG Payless), 236 *(planting supplies, ©Dzioebk)*, 240 (©Jane Rix), 241, *(grass/terrarium, ©Africa Studio; cacti/terrarium/cacti, ©Armei Studio)*, 242 (©Robyn Mackenzie), 245 *(sweet potato vine, ©Sony Ho)*, 248 *(parade, ©Dale A Stork)*, 249 (©sonya etchison), 253 *(service dog, ©Jeroen van den Broek; rescue dog, ©Jim Parkin)*, 254 *(therapy dog, ©Monkey Business Images)*, 276 (©Lorraine Swanson), 281 (©Steve Bower), 285 *(football players, ©Michael Chamberlin)*, 292 *(showerhead, ©ThamKC)*, and 310 (©Denise LeBlanc)

U.S. Mint, courtesy—pages 109–110, 111 *(coins with mint marks)*, 112 *(coins)*, 114–116, 117 *(United States Golden Dollar Coin obverse featuring Sacagawea ©1999 United States Mint. All Rights Reserved. Used with permission.)*, and 117 *(all other coin images)*

Notes

Notes

Notes

THE OUTDOOR CODE

As an American, I will do my best to—

- ◆ Be clean in my outdoor manners,
- ◆ Be careful with fire,
- ◆ Be considerate in the outdoors, and
- ◆ Be conservation minded.

LEAVE NO TRACE*
PRINCIPLES FOR KIDS

Know Before You Go

Choose the Right Path

Trash Your Trash

Leave What You Find

Be Careful With Fire

Respect Wildlife

Be Kind to Other Visitors

*The member-driven Leave No Trace Center for Outdoor Ethics teaches people how to enjoy the outdoors responsibly. This copyrighted information has been reprinted with permission from the Leave No Trace Center for Outdoor Ethics: www.LNT.org.